MISSION IMPOSSIBLE?

MISSION IMPOSSIBLE?

by
Peter Sedgwick

Collins
FLAME

First published in Great Britain in 1990 under the Flame
imprint by Collins Religious Division, part of the Collins
Publishing Group, 8 Grafton Street London W1X 3LD

Copyright © Peter Sedgwick 1990
ISBN 0 00 599206 0

Typeset by K.G. Farren, Scarborough
Printed and bound in Great Britain by
Bell and Bain Ltd, Glasgow

Conditions of Sale
This book is sold subject to the condition
that it shall not, by way of trade or otherwise,
be lent, re-sold, hired out or otherwise circulated
without the publisher's prior consent in any form of
binding or cover other than that in which it is
published and without a similar condition
including this condition being imposed
on the subsequent purchaser

CONTENTS

Introduction		7
Chapter 1	**A Tale of Three Churches**	11
	St Mary the Virgin, Monkseaton	16
	The Star Centre, Newcastle – the Epiphany Team Parish, North Gosforth	29
	Ascension Outreach Project, North Kenton	41
	Conclusion	48
Chapter 2	**What is Mission?**	50
	Secularization	52
	The New Testament Church	60
	The Local Church and Mission	65
	Conclusion	71
Chapter 3	**Rejecting God**	73
	Sunderland and Scotswood	75
	Youth	85
	Suburbia	93
	Summary: Great Britain	96
	The European Dimension	98
Chapter 4	**Personal Evangelism**	104
	The End of Religious Tribalism	104
	Public Faith	108
	The Attractiveness of Christianity	111
	The Response to God	115
	A Criticism of Mass Evangelism	122
	Conclusion	131
Chapter 5	**Industrial Mission**	135
	The Closure of Consett	136
	The Changes in Industrial Mission	142
	Industrial Mission and Mission	145
Chapter 6	**Pastoral Care and Unity**	159
	Introduction	160
	Deprivation in the Community	163
	Lay Ministry	169

	The Experience of Women	173
	Unity and Mission	177
	Conclusion	183
Conclusion		184
Notes		188

INTRODUCTION

This small book is about mission in England in the 1980s. It is based on my experiences as a Theological Consultant to the churches in the North-East of England from 1982 to 1988. There is a common pattern to most of the six chapters. I have tried to look at what is wrong in each situation, then to see how people tried to change it, and to think theologically about it. The names of the towns and villages, suburbs and industries, are local to the North-East, but I hope the study is of some value elsewhere.

Equally the book has a pattern running throughout it. I have begun with three examples of local change in our understanding of prayer, of social action and of evangelism. Only then do I try in the second chapter to define how mission might be seen as part of the Christian faith. This leads into the issues of evangelism, of the world of work and of pastoral care and Christian unity. Personal despair and a divided Church are strong witnesses against taking a missionary Church seriously; stories of compassion and experiences of reconciliation work equally strongly the other way.

In the end of the day mission concerns the relationship of the local church to the community around it, and beyond that its responsibility to the world. Its task is not to take Christ to the world. Christ is there in His Church and in His world. Our problem is a blindness of imagination, from which we may well pray to be delivered.[1] In Barth's famous words, "A man without imagination is more of an invalid than one who lacks a leg." But the blindness is corporate, and it afflicts us all. So Elisha prayed for his servant, who was afraid and did not know how to act, "Open his eyes that he might see." And the young man saw the mountain full of horses and chariots of fire around Elisha. It is not only in films that we need our imagination lifting to see the chariots of fire. The mission of the Church exists because with our imagination re-awakened we have no alternative but to act the way we do.

This book is not about how to "do evangelism", run a successful church or tell others about past successes. It is not about how to do anything. Too many books on mission presuppose that if the technique is correct, then the rest will follow. Instead this book argues that the theology of mission is all important. Without it, evangelism, social concern and action; Industrial Mission; spirituality; and ecumenism will all fly apart. Where they do not do that, it is in practice often due to the personality of one person who holds it all together in his or her ministry. Yet only a proper theology can actually give meaning and purpose to each of these activities, both on their own and when taken together. A theology of mission is not set apart from the day-to-day life of the church: it is, so this book argues, a theology which must be worked out in conjunction with the local church.

Therefore, academic theology is in dialogue with the experience of the local church. Both express the presence of the Spirit, the divine wisdom; both draw upon the worship of God in Jesus Christ.

> Nothing can so effectively deaden the moral sense and darken the light of reason as religion – when religion has turned from the living God to worship a stone. What the living God requires of His worshippers is not defence, but the trust that follows where He leads. The idol is comfortably familiar; the living God is old but ever new; and they also would know Him must be ready for the unexpected. They must be ready to see God act in strange ways and hear Him speak in unaccustomed tones.[2]

These meditations by John Burnaby on Good Friday are equally relevant to a theology of mission. The dialogue of academic theology with the very local, concrete and immediate has as its goal the understanding of mission in contemporary England. There is no reason to expect a theology of mission to be an endorsement of the familiar, accustomed patterns of behaviour. A living tradition develops in new ways, but when you lose tradition (as a friend once said to me), you are left with heritage. The mission of the Church is not heritage. Much in this book examines the decay of a living tradition into heritage. A theology of mission is an attempt to discover where the tradition of the Church points, often unexpectedly, in future decades. This book is therefore not theology from the grass roots: it is too much set in academic patterns of thought for that. Yet it is not what it has turned out to be as if the history of many local churches in the region did not matter. Only because I have been and heard dozens of churches discuss, and act upon, their theology of mission, could these chapters have been written. Above all it is the experiences of the conversations in the Theological Consultancy which make these reflections possible. Their honesty, realism and Christian commitment lie behind this book.

I owe a debt of thanks to many people. During the six years I worked as Theological Consultant to the North-East Ecumenical Group (the Church leaders in the region) I met clergy and laity in all walks of life and in all the denominations. My greatest gratitude is to the members of the Consultancy, and to their Chairman, the Very Rev. Peter Baelz, Dean of Durham. Next I owe much to the support of the Church leaders, and to their Secretary, the Rev. Keith Huxley. There are many parish clergy whom I could mention: some of their names occur in this book, and I am privileged to have worked with them. In particular I should mention the Rev. John Stevinson, the Durham Diocesan Secretary to the Board for Mission and Unity, for his support and many valuable conversations on mission. I should also thank Canon James Anderson, of the Church of England's Board for Mission and Unity, and the Rev. Chris Beales of the Industrial Committee, who made helpful comments on an early draft of this book. Several theologians in Durham and Newcastle also contributed much to the work of the Consultancy: Canon Dan Hardy and Canon Stephen Sykes were members of the Consultancy; Dr Richard Roberts and Fr Colin Carr were not, but I owe them all an enormous debt for their insight. This study originally arose as part of a Christian Studies course drawn up for the Diocese of Newcastle by the North of England Institute for Christian Education. The co-operation of Mrs Elizabeth Fisher and the Rev. Dr Jeff Astley of NEICE provided the initial impetus for drawing together my thoughts on mission, for which I am very grateful. I am grateful to Mrs Gill Fincham, my secretary, for her skills in typing this manuscript. Above all else it is the friendship of so many people, inside and outside the churches, which I remember from this time. I will remember the time spent as Theological Consultant as a special time; not least because of the help and influence of Peter Baelz, and the support of my wife.

---

1. Bishop of Newcastle, Presidential Address to Newcastle Diocesan Synod, 25 October 1986.
2. J. Burnaby, "Forgiveness in Christ", *Good Friday at St Margaret's*, Mowbrays 1957, p. 136.

CHAPTER 1

A Tale of Three Churches

I said, Ah! what shall I write?
I inquired up and down.
   (He's tricked me before
with his manifold lurking-places.)
I looked for His symbol at the door.
I have looked for a long while
   at the textures and contours.
I have run a hand over the trivial intersections.
I have journeyed among the dead forms
   causation projects from pillar to pylon.
I have tired the eyes of the mind
   regarding the colours and lights.
I have felt for His wounds
   in nozzles and containers.
I have wondered for the automatic devices.
I have tested the inane patterns
   without prejudice.
I have been on my guard
   not to condemn the unfamiliar.
For it is easy to miss Him
   at the turn of a civilization.

I have watched the wheels go round in case I might see the living creatures like the appearance of lamps, in case I might see the Living God projected from the Machine. I have said to the perfected steel, be my sister and for the glassy towers I thought I felt some beginnings of His creature, but A, a, a, Domine Deus, my hands found the glazed work unrefined and the terrible crystal a stage-paste . . . Eia Domine Deus.

David Jones, "A, a, a, Domine Deus"

Mission Impossible?   *A Tale of Three Churches*

"A theology of mission will be contextual: it will be an attempt to work out what people believe, why they believe in it, and the implications of what they believe. This will be rooted in some context or another." Such was a letter from Fr Jim O'Keefe in 1986 about how the Church might reflect on what it thought it was doing.

This book is an attempt to listen to a series of people, parishes and groups thinking about what they believe, why they believe in it and what the implications of all this might be. It is based on the experience of the Theological Consultancy in the North-East of England from 1982 to 1988. This group, chaired by the Dean of Durham, Peter Baelz, was made up of parish clergy from all denominations, lay people, academics and myself. The task of the group was to help the Christian churches in the North-East in their mission to the people and institutions around them. Yet it was not offering practical help. It aimed to help by making a parish, industrial mission or any other group conscious of why it was acting that way: in other words, it involved thinking about the local situation in a theological way.

Therefore any book about mission should be devoted to explaining what that last sentence means. But what might a local situation involve? For six years it involved work with an inner-city parish which started a centre for people in need as a resource for a neighbourhood with high unemployment next to an affluent middle-class parish: the work of the Star Centre in St Mary's parish, Fawdon, Newcastle. It involved the development by a large, suburban parish of lay ministry, of small groups concerned with evangelism and above all of a place to be quiet and pray, high in the Cheviot Hills of Northumberland: the work of the hermitage at Shepherd's Law, Northumberland, and the parish of St Mary's, Monkseaton, Whitley Bay. It involved placing two Church Army sisters on a deprived estate to live there with a brief for evangelism, tenants' action and the building of a congregation on that estate, where none existed before: the work of the Ascension Outreach in the parish of The Ascension, North Kenton, Newcastle.

Other illustrations will occur in the book. But these three examples, all set in one city in the North-East, show the different ways in which mission can be understood by the local church. It can mean social concern and identification with local people; it can mean evangelism in an area where hardly anyone attends the local parish church; it can mean a spirituality of silence, meditation and waiting upon God. All three involve the local church both working with the people around it and building up the resources of the congregation. Each parish seeks both to grow in numbers and to be faithful to the Gospel, yet also to be part of the local community. They are very diverse areas in one city in the region. Above all each parish responds to a need which is seen by the parish to be important that it meets.

God does not impose His will upon parishes, so that there is no possibility of any other action. There is always the possibility of not discovering where the call of God lies for that parish, or of assuming that the Christian way is known already by the congregation. The call of God is to be faithful to the relationship with God – no more, no less. How that relationship is to be understood is shown not in abstract doctrine, but in belonging to a group of people who have been affected by the presence of a mystery which they call "God". By belonging to that group we see in the lives of others the presence of a God who gives both promises and demands. In the lives of "Saints" and of fellow-Christians with much imperfection like ourselves we see what talk of the purposes of God might mean.

Once we seek to discover that relationship, and become, however tentatively, part of a people which lives with the memory of the life of Christ, we have to discover the implications of the relationship. This is done by seeking to find the greatest needs of the people who are called to follow God – the congregation – and the greatest needs of the community around them. Central to this book is the belief that this cannot be determined beforehand, so that you can say "action with the poor" or "preaching the Gospel" or whatever. Rather it is by looking at the local congregation and the local community, each with their own integrity, that the possibility of our developing the relationship with God occurs. The relationship is portrayed in a fundamental way in the events displayed in the Scriptures, but it must itself be worked out in the present day.

Therefore this first chapter looks at three examples of local mission because they are concrete examples of what mission means: lived stories, to employ a term much used in current talk about the nature of belief in God today. Each of these examples grows out of a relationship with God which the participants sought to enter into. Each then involves finding what might be the possibility of acting in a way which would be faithful to that relationship. Each next involves carrying out that possibility of action in practice in a confusing, fragmented and very active modern city. Finally, and perhaps most important of all, there must be the reflection on where that action – with all its talk, planning and taking of decisions – has actually led to. What do we now think of where we are in the world; what have we learnt about ourselves; what have we learnt about our relationship with God?

It is important to notice what is not being claimed here. Contrary to much recent writing about mission, an experience of personal salvation which is intense and particular is not essential. It may be valuable for many, but as Stanley Hauerwas puts it:

> To locate ourselves within that history and people does not mean we must have some special experience of personal salvation. Redemption, rather, is a change in which we accept the invitation to become part of God's Kingdom, a Kingdom through which we acquire a character befitting one who has heard God's call. Now an intense personal experience may be important for many but such experiences cannot in themselves

be substitutes for learning to find the significance of our lives only in God's ongoing journey with creation.[1]

Learning to find the significance of our lives – that is what the three examples of mission given in this chapter are all about. Later chapters will attempt to ask what mission is and why churches might grow or decline; what is the relationship of worship and mission; what are questions of evangelism, Industrial Mission, pastoral care, unity between churches and the worldwide Church. But before any of this it is important that the reality of local attempts to listen to each other, inside and outside the church, are understood, and what that listening means in terms of meeting the religious and social needs which that listening involved. Personal experience of God is much prized in some religious traditions – "being with the Lord". Others find the language alien, forcing them to lay claim to an experience they do not themselves have. Behind both groups is the placing of our lives within a history and a people which is shaped by the reality of God. In that placing, however it is worked out, there will be the beginning of a relationship with God; the possibility of action; the action itself in response to the needs of the community and of the Church; and reflection on that action. In all of this we seek to learn what it means to be faithful to the belief that we are all God's creatures, and to learn the skills to be faithful. Such learning is often made easiest by looking at how others have learnt to trust God. Therefore in an attempt to answer what it means to say that people believe, why they believe and what are the implications of what they believe (the challenge of Jim O'Keefe's letter, with which this chapter began), I begin with these examples from Newcastle in the 1980s. Needless to say, there are many others which could be given: these are simply three with which I was involved.

St Mary the Virgin, Monkseaton

In this parish, there was a long tradition of churchgoing. The congregation was large, and was probably one of the biggest in Newcastle Diocese. There was much to give thanks for. The church building was well laid out, and in good repair; the church was well endowed, with a well-housed clergy; there was a constant supply of clergy. Many parishes would find themselves very fortunate to be in such a position without anything obviously to complain or worry about. Thus there was no need for fundraising, or building ventures; of course there was always the pressure of supporting the diocese financially, and that was not to be underestimated, but it was a comparatively wealthy area.

That meant, as the parish priest, John Lowen, pointed out to his congregation, that there was nothing to stand in the way of the main task of the Church in this suburban area. But what was that task, and what prevented the Church fulfilling it in that area? The parish thought about its priorities, but also about its failings which prevented the relationship with God deepening for many people.

First, there were decades of dependence by congregations upon priests and institutions. In the past, when many parishes were large and could employ several priests, that dependence could be sustained, even if it might lead to clericalism. Now, with a diminishing Christian presence in a secular society, such an option was no longer viable. Related to this was the tendency of some individuals to feel that their own inadequacy in expressing belief or sense of unworthiness, from whatever inner motive, meant that they had to depend on their parish priest for complete inspiration and guidance – much as a shattered body depends on a life-support machine. Those who were committed to the congregation also tended to equate their commitment with membership of a particular group, such as the choir or Mothers' Union, or with a particular friendship. Thus clubs, jobs, persons tended to displace commitment to the following of God, as seen in Christ. Instead of reinforcing commitment, they displaced it by making commitment dependent on a pre-defined small group, a cause or a person.

Thus behind the life of an affluent, well-ordered congregation (in terms of buildings, etc.) there lay what was called "an unhealthy, self-absorbed and jumpy community". "Much energy and effort is expended to get precisely nowhere" in pastoral relationships: a game seen as "ludicrous" and "terribly damaging – utterly destructive of trust, love, true pastoral work and our corporate life". These hard words of the parish priest were not spoken without much consultation with the congregation. But they were on the whole accepted by them, and led inevitably to the fact that more money, more priests and further social events would not lead the parish to be more effective in mission – in any way whatsoever.

Thus the recovery of a true spirituality and the development of lay ministry went hand in hand. Yet there was much outside the congregation that also made the growth of spirituality difficult. Faith was seen as a personal thing, or as something which you were born into and remained with – this was the prevailing social belief. The surburban lifestyle was active where many residents had recently arrived. There was, and still is, a sense of social achievement in belonging to this suburb. This led to a very individualistic community. Although there were many social activities in Monkseaton, it was also a place which laid great stress on privacy, and on achieving individual goals and ambitions. Freedom to make one's mark was all important: it was the sense of keeping options open, of not being constrained, of being one's own master. At the same time there was a heavy burden of responsibility carried home from work, in a region where the struggle was to preserve employment and prevent manufacturing industry contracting further. Thus the failure to be successful at work was not just a personal failure, for it carried with it implications for others' welfare. Less orders for the firm meant more unemployment for others.

St Mary's, Monkseaton, was not unusual in being a parish apparently well endowed, but with much personal manipulation inside the life of the congregation and much fragmented community life outside it. Many parishes suffer from the same frenetic activity, the same commitment to personal self-sufficiency at all costs whatever the deception involved (often quite unconsciously), the same inability to be what they are there for. What was unusual was the degree of analysis which the parish carried out. For this parish, more projects in inner-city areas would each be just one more project, with even greater activity and even less attention to the exploration of what the real needs were.

Thus the parish began to seek to find the correct priorities. They came to feel that there were two: the search for a proper form of spirituality, which could represent an authentic peace, silence and rest in the midst of such frenetic activity, and the growth of responsibility for the life of the parish by the congregation itself. Only out of both these could the church hope to offer something to the suburban community around it, without running the risk of equating Christian mission with ever greater activity. Therefore the parish began to consider what spirituality and mission might mean.

Spirituality is often associated with pious behaviour and religious disciplines, which lead to particular practices in communities, such as fasting, going on retreats, etc. Alternatively it can be seen as linked to a counter-culture which protests against the materialist rat-race of modern life, but is again foreign to much of suburban existence. This community called itself quite "religious", but defined this term in a particular, cultural way. This religiosity has no place for a counter-culture or for religious discipline.

Writing about the spirituality of the proposed venture at Shepherd's Law, John Lowen knew that Christians often associated the contemplative life with an escape from the real world, which was unhealthy and introspective. However, it was easy for active busy Christians to "forget God in the midst of well-meaning activity". The parish therefore found the request of a hermit for help something of a surprise. Although members of the congregation were experts on the needs of society, and understood industry or high finance, they had not expected to be asked for help by a monk. He spoke of his hope of establishing a small contemplative community at Shepherd's Law, which would be a place of sanctuary for those who felt broken and wounded. It was not just a place of peace and quiet, but a place where by waiting upon God the community could pray for all those who had forgotten God. Christians, he argued, did not only need peace and stillness, but also needed to be prayed for and taught by example – for they were the people most likely to forget God by good deeds. It is the same theme as was argued for earlier in this chapter, where mission only arises out of an exploration of what God is calling people to do. It is not one more activity; or one more project. It cannot be pre-defined at all.

The reaction of the parish to the hermit, called Brother Harold, was very human.

> We were unused to silence, contemplative prayer and hermits, and Brother Harold came upon us like something out of a sketch by John Cleese. Feelings of puzzlement, embarrassment and curiosity were evident. We wondered whether such a venture was either practical or even desirable in this day and age. To some it sounded simply odd and foolish. To others the risks attached to it were too great: where would the other members of such a community come from? Would anyone come, or would we be left with a rebuilt folly? Would Brother Harold die and the Franciscans and other orders find the building useless? Could the building even be built, could it be heated, would anyone see any point to it, even if it could be done?

There were, and are, no answers to this response. The vision was, however, about the possibility of acting in a way faithful to the relationship of the parish with God. It spoke directly to the needs of the congregation, to strive for silence and peace in the midst not only of frenetic activity but of fragmentation, power games, divided selves and a belief that only personal freedom mattered, which was a freedom to choose more activity and not be bound by the constraints of the past.

The vision was also about what it meant to be a people, or a community, who are aware of a past history where "God" has been real to that community. In brief, it meant returning to a tradition not for its own sake but to see the faithfulness of God to His people and their gathering here and there in small groups into a church. The tradition was not valuable just for itself, but because it showed how to make sense of life, what the way to inner worth and significance was and how to find our story in the story of God's people.

So around the site of the hermitage were the earliest roots of Northern Christianity. The great names of the past, such as Cuthbert, Bede, Oswald and Aidan, were not far away, at Lindisfarne, Jarrow and Hexham. The vision was one of prayer, of teaching about prayer and of existence in the contemporary world with some rootedness in a given silence. Therefore, in a way quite out of the normal pattern of parish life, Brother Harold suggested that people might like to leave their ordinary life for a few days to learn to be still before God, not in a religious community such as a monastery or retreat house with set ways of behaviour, but in a solitary place. Shepherd's Law is high up on the moors, in a wild, ruined farm, with some trees which struggle against the wind. There are many species of wildlife and plants, and a great feeling of loneliness.

Brother Harold suggested building four self-contained cells linked to his own hermitage. The parish finally agreed to the request, building began, and people began to visit the hermitage. It was an unlikely project for a parish concerned with the needs of society. Yet the building went on. There were setbacks. There was, unexpectedly, criticism from other parish clergy, who could not see the point of the project. But the parish adopted Shepherd's Law, and realized that although finance and building were important, it was not just one more project. As important was the occasional presence of the hermit, Brother Harold, preaching and teaching the congregation, before going back to his hermitage. The tradition, with all its roots and its evocation of the Northern Saints in the simple chapel at Shepherd's Law by icon and picture, is thus related to the modern world. For the tradition is only there to teach the primacy of prayer in the Church's service to the world. Even the openness to God in prayer, self-justifying though it is, only leads on to expose the need for some balance to a life where freedom is an end in itself; where there are always choices to be made about situations which we do not control; where there is no inner harmony.

Finding "the significance of our lives only in God's ongoing journey with creation" is therefore the reason why Shepherd's Law became important in Monkseaton, which is a very different place from the high Northumbrian moorland. But what has this to do with mission? Out of the commitment to build Shepherd's Law and to discover the life of prayer (and the two are synonymous) came an interest in lay ministry and in helping the mentally ill.

In June 1988 a parish consultation took place under Canon Bob Langley of Newcastle Cathedral. It was attended by some sixty-five people. He noticed that the church was still introspective, and the comments made on the day did not concern the wider aspects of the Kingdom of God, as proclaimed by Jesus. Equally he observed the vagueness of the prospects which the day had thrown up. Nevertheless, there were proposals, and the congregation was aware of the need to take more responsibility for itself; to seek spiritual resources alongside the need for evangelism and social concern; and to be prepared to experiment in worship.

In practice this meant dividing the parish into small contact groups, with a cellular structure. The purpose of these groups was set out in a parish document. With fifty or so groups, there was bound to be diversity, but nevertheless the aims were reasonably similar for each:

SOCIAL bringing 8–10 people together three or four times a year in a home. These meetings would be informal, allowing people to get to know each other and breaking down the barriers we have at present between the three morning congregations. Newcomers could easily be slotted into a suitable group.

PASTORAL In between meetings, the leader and others in the group would keep an eye out for anyone who was ill or in any kind of trouble. Some leaders would want to visit themselves while others would inform the clergy or the pastoral visitors scheme.

COMMUNICATION As well as getting information directly to each member of the congregation, the groups would be invaluable wherever a sounding of the parish's mind on an important new direction for St Mary's was required.

SPIRITUAL Once people got to know each other, they might wish to pray together using something like the Lent Groups' pack on prayer, where necessary. Some groups might combine to form groups for Lent; the informal atmosphere should help people to discuss their faith openly and honestly, sharing doubts as well as certainties.

MISSION The meeting of the 50 or so groups should have some impact on the parish; beyond this some groups may want to share Christ with non-members in a variety of ways.

Such a division of the parish into small groups presupposes that the ordained ministry is part of a team. Paul's reflection on the Body of Christ in 1 Corinthians 12 leads him to a view of the Church as made up of varieties of gifts, varieties of service, but all knit together by baptism and by the inspiration of the Spirit. Equally, in view of the dependency of the congregation referred to earlier and the difficulty of achieving mature relationships within the congregation, the vision of Paul is one of mutual caring: "that the members may have the same care for one another. If one member suffers, all suffer together."

Robin Greenwood's recent book *Reclaiming the Church* takes up the theme of the vocation of each baptized person within the Church. The function of the ordained ministry is to lead from within. He writes that

> to be "apostolic" means that the whole church . . . must be seen to be a community living radically as Servants of Christ, in and for the world, constantly asking the question: "If that's what Jesus and the apostles were saying and doing, what should we be saying and doing?" The church needs therefore, to be daily placing its life under the judgement of the word of Jesus Christ, present through his Spirit to his community today. The ordained minister needs to be one chosen because he or she has the gifts, resources and wisdom constantly to represent the mind of Christ in the church, as it were holding up a mirror of the Gospel to the congregation and asking "Are we a true community of Jesus?"[2]

Equally Anthony Hanson has argued for the equal responsibility of clergy and laity for the ministry of the Church in the world.

> If this church, despite all its sins, can yet be described as the body of Christ in the Pauline sense, the ministry has no right to look beyond it to some more holy or more authoritative body to which it is (in Christ) responsible. From this it follows

that the whole church, not just the ordained part of it, has responsibility for the Church's life and activity in the world. Hence the laity not only may be, but ought to be associated with the clergy in all matters of faith, discipline and morals.[3]

Hanson correctly argues that the outworking of his principle in practice will vary from culture to culture, but the issue is straightforward. All priesthood stems from the priesthood of Christ. Ordained (clerical) priesthood only is an instrument or focus of the Church's priesthood, which itself is from Christ. The ordained ministry has a different priesthood from ordinary Christians, but it is not separate from it either. All Christians share in Christ's priesthood by belonging to the church in baptism. Ordained priesthood only focuses and represents the Church's priesthood: it is never a substitute for it, nor can it act in its place. And priesthood, which is not an easy term to use in a secular society, comes ultimately from the love and self-giving of Christ: "For the Son of Man also came not to be served but to serve, and to give his life as a ransom for many." Christian priesthood, then, is service on behalf of others in Christ's name.

Lay ministry is not simply about the leadership of groups. St Mary's has evolved a pattern where most of the day-to-day tasks of the parish – administration, finance, magazine, youth work and children's work – are now run by lay people. Above all the majority of sick communions, where those sick at home are taken Holy Communion, are now administered by members of the congregation licensed by the Bishop. When Justin Martyr in AD 150 wrote in his "First Apology" of the communion being taken out to the parish by deacons, he meant members of the congregation chosen by the rest of the congregation and approved of by the Bishop. The benefit for a twentieth-century congregation is that they can relate the mysterious primacy of the living God to the action of God upon those who need His mercy and love. It does not have to be a priest who enables this relationship to be made. The taking of bread and wine by a priest is within the tradition of the Church: in celebrating the communion God is asked to be faithful to His promise to offer us His life, to quote the parish priest again. But at the administration of the consecreated bread and wine to someone sick at home, the relationship is between the sick person and God Himself. Thus the focus shifts from the celebrant, who may be a familiar vicar or curate, on to the action of the celebration and what is celebrated. Again John Lowen points out that this demands far more faith, for the relationship must now be between God (in the action of celebration) and the believer, not simply between the believer and God's representative. Yet equally unleavened bread is bread for a pilgrimage, a journey, which does not take up space or go stale. So, symbolically the unleavened bread speaks of the collective pilgrimage of that community which is the Church. That community is made up of all those who belong within it.

> And yet, paradoxically almost, not only does this method of administration highlight that it is God and God alone who acts to save – it emphasizes, at the same time, that all Christians, not just their priests, are called to be the bearers of Christ's life and love. It stresses the great truth that we are all called to live His risen life and show it to others. For although it is true that God and God alone acts, originates and gives life; it is equally true that He wishes all people and indeed all His creation to be fully alive with that life.

This sermon by John Lowen highlights the missionary emphasis of shared ministry. Equally the church began experimenting once every other month with a service without communion at their main 9.15 service. For a parish with a strong tradition of Catholic spirituality, this was felt as a truly major change by many worshippers. Yet many people feel hesitant enough about formal worship: formal worship where they do not receive communion, being unconfirmed, only strengthens this isolation. The link between Shepherd's Law and the parish was not simply a strengthening of existing patterns of worship: it could set the parish free from them as well.

Peter Baelz and Michael Gaudoin-Parker wrote on the theology of communion by extension for the Theological Consultancy, at the request of some local churches, in April 1987. Peter Baelz saw Christ as the primary and normative sacrament in His person and character, expressed in word and deed. Words and deeds were sacramental symbols, for they held together the natural and the transcendent: "passports for traffic across the boundary" of this world and the eternal. Yet the significance of the symbol was real, not ideal, for it has its source and authority in the being and activity of God. The danger of taking bread and wine as "things" in themselves, apart from the action of celebrating the communion service, was that they became imbued with notions of magic and "supernatural" power. Yet if the symbolic significance of the sacrament was placed in the mind of the believer, then the reality of the bread and wine ceased to matter. An adequate sacramental theology would take up the reality of God's action and give it a meaning which was personal but not arbitrary; it would be placed in a context of meaning, so that the symbol drew on a universe of shared beliefs and values; therefore the symbolism of communion by extension would be one which "possess[ed] an elasticity of meaning without being formless or arbitrary . . . more like living ideas than abstract concepts."

Similarly Michael Gaudoin-Parker speaks of the sacraments as "visible words", quoting Augustine, of the divine Love speaking of the restoration of creation and its possession by God's own presence. Thus natural, material things are shaped by the creative word of God, and transfigured as the ordinary stuff of daily experience with divine potential as symbols of love, fellowship and community. We will return to these ideas in Chapter 4, when Vanstone's and Hauerwas's theologies of the Church are examined. Michael Gaudoin-Parker, as a Roman Catholic priest and theologian, draws on the documents of the Second Vatican Council, especially *Lumen gentium*, the document on the

Church. Here the place of all Christians in the mission of the Church is spelt out: they "must carry their witness of Christ all over the world . . . a readiness to undertake the variety of works and duties which advance the renewal and the extension of the building of the Church."

Neither writer advocated treating the communion of the sick and house-bound by lay people as replacing the action of the ordained minister in celebrating the communion service. Yet once the wider significance of these symbols is seen as "passports for traffic across the boundary" (Baelz) or "doors of perception of the new creation of the Risen Lord, who re-interprets the struggle and pain, frustrations, disappointments, and tragedy of our journey in life" (Gaudoin-Parker), then the way is open to new patterns of ministry and new experiments in worship.

And so finally to social involvement. The danger here was of one more project which would take up the energy of the parish. Throughout the whole development of a new direction for the parish, the emphasis was on waiting on God; self-reflection; listening to the needs of others. Out of this came one initiative which expressed the need to serve the local community. There was, and is, a serious shortage of accommodation in the community where patients recovering from mental illness could be supported. Some would always need live-in support; some would eventually attain complete independence. The Social Services Department lacked the capital funds to set up the project: it was here that St Mary's Church felt that they could use their wealth to help.

Thus the parish tried to use their wealth as creatively as possible. It was not a project which they would run or own: the dangers of patronizing those more disadvantaged were avoided. But equally the role of St Mary's in funding two community houses would be enormous. As Social Services paid a rental on the church investment, therefore in time the parish would be able to capitalize a further venture.

This project is still developing, as Shepherd's Law approaches completion. What is the relationship of spirituality, silence and psychiatric care? The relationship turns on the meaning of the term "dependence". St Mary's was a dependent congregation: it had been taught to be priest-dependent across the generations. Shepherd's Law embodied a vision of the individual empowered by waiting upon God; where true dependence on the God who frees His people for joy and service allows a spirituality that is honest, sometimes abrasive, and allows personal independence alongside mutual interdependence. Those ill with mental disorder become dependent on institutions, other people and their own fantasies. If a parish which wished to help the local community without dominating it – providing the eighteenth camel in the famous Sufi parable – could assist those most in need, then it would serve those seeking their own independence while at the same time working out the implications of what it meant to be set free in Christ. Spiritual freedom entails an end to dependence upon other human beings, and a striving towards interdependence: social freedom entails an end to set patterns of human living, often within institutions. Together spiritual freedom and social freedom run into one another: without a common equality and dependence upon God, the parish and those leaving hospital become worlds apart. "If I give away all I have, and if I deliver my body to be burned, but if I have no love I gain nothing." What is significant about this passage is that it follows on directly from Paul's emphasis on shared ministry. There is no division in a theology of mission between the shared ministry of each Christian and the service of the world.

Finally, it is worth returning to Shepherd's Law and its remoteness. David Isitt's comment on the desert tradition and the Early Christian Desert Fathers is salutary: he argues that there is too much written about the desert as a place of purity where, romantically, the individual can meet God.

We are told that we all need to find our own desert place, so that God may find us there. Well, possibly. It may be true that the Jews, from a later standpoint, came to look back at the desert as the place where their experience of God was pristine and uncorrupt. It is certainly true that Christians have been inclined to imitate Christ in withdrawing to remote places for prayer and reflections. But it's also true that the Jews were quite unidealistic about their desert places. You have only to stand on the Mount of Olives and look east into the Wilderness of Judea to know what a "howling waste" is. The desert, in Jewish imagery is a place of danger where evil spirits and obscene creatures abound. It's not a lovely unpolluted place you can escape to, but a place where you confront evil out of a need to be delivered from it. The saints of the Egyptian desert certainly knew that.[4]

You confront evil out of a need to be delivered from it. It is probably true of the situation in many middle-class, apparently successful parishes: the evils of dependence; wealth and status; emotional manipulation; fear of the future. Only through these burdens, which are often the fault of no one individual but are the shadow side of the community in all its weight of past, half-forgotten teaching, lies the way to mission and evangelism. "For freedom Christ has set us free; stand fast therefore, and do not submit again to a yoke of slavery" (Galations 5:1). Freedom restores the living tradition of the Church from a slow decay into a (very English) heritage. Yet freedom may involve re-examining the teaching of the past in order that the burdens of dependence and status may be released.

The Star Centre, Newcastle – the Epiphany Team Parish, North Gosforth

The Star Centre is housed in a disused teachers' centre on an estate in North Newcastle. The area is a mixture of private and council estates, with pockets of very high unemployment. The name Star is derived from the initials S.T.A.R. – Skills, Training, Action and Resources. Local community groups are beginning to use it – a Baptist church, a job club, a charity shop, a history society. A coffee bar/lunch club, a centre for the mentally ill, a teenage girls' club and some self-employed businessmen are established. A local school is helping to decorate the premises, and local churches and a synagogue have funded the initial salary of the project and community worker. So too have the Church Urban Fund (through Northern Rock) and the British Council of Churches. The emphasis is firmly on listening to the local people: telling those involved with the centre what is required. This meant a slow start, without great initiatives which might swamp local feelings. There has been a series of open meetings in the evenings with fifty or more present. The area has many young people, single-parent families and patches of unemployment which go up to 35 per cent of the adult workforce. Yet it is close to prosperous areas such as Gosforth.

There is a small group of Christians and others who have been involved with the Centre for over eighteen months. They include a Jewish rabbi and some of no (or unrelated) religious allegiance. It was this group which met on a number of evenings to look at issues of social concern, in relation to their religious faith. In particular, they related the vision of the Centre to their faith, or lack of it. And most particularly of all, they looked at the links between social justice and what has been called in traditional Protestant language "justification": the experience of being accepted by God and having been forgiven.

What reasons did this group give for being involved in this project? May spoke of Christianity providing an end to guilt, and a new relationship with God. Her previous job (she was now retired) had taken her as a DHSS employee into contact with drug addicts, prostitutes, meths drinkers and criminals at Tyne Dock. They were all human, they were warm and friendly, but in their humanity they still missed "the best" – the living experience of joy, peace and thankfulness with God. Christianity was not an obvious part of their life. It wasn't either that all churchgoers experience this salvation. Many Christians did good works from a sense of duty. Muriel commented that this sense of purpose and fulfilment could often be found in those who did "good works". It could be a relic of past churchgoing. It could occupy the time in those middle years. Peter suggested that it could be a form of therapy.

The group therefore distinguished between on the one hand what May called "salvation" – inner peace with God; the sense of duty; motivation for caring for others – and on the other hand satisfaction in doing something worthwhile. Peter felt that Christianity for him was love of neighbour; living with a Christian responsibility in the world; and stewardship of God's gifts. This was Christian witness, even to people who did not know he was a Christian. He hoped people saw something in the motivation of Christians which was attractive, even if people didn't say it was religious. Peter stressed that the Star Centre facilities could not be "laid on": it had to respond to the underlying needs of loneliness, lack of meaning, lack of warmth. The press played up bad news, ignoring the caring attitude of many young people. The Star Centre was not there to patronize the unemployed, elderly or lonely, but to enable them to be themselves. Muriel noted the lack of facilities on the North Kenton Estate, near Gosforth: the loss of relatives who had once lived nearby in the inner city; the boredom of young people; the incipient depression. The opportunity was there for the churches if they would but take it. Yet they must always listen to those who had lived there for years.

The group looked at the way North-East communities had existed forty years ago. Hardship then inspired generosity to others. The breakup of communities led to an "I'm all right Jack" attitude. There was also, said May, a dependence on the Welfare State. People felt someone else – or the government – would take over. Richard said that "the church" was often seen to be middle-class, and lacking in credibility today. George also noted how politicized the whole area was: churches and Scout groups were not popular groups for help from community funds in the eyes of local politicians. In the older parts of the city things were very different. Much community involvement on the outer estates such as Fawdon and North Kenton was for political ends. He was disappointed that the Star Centre had not attracted more unemployed people yet. The job club catered for only a few. Hilda and Muriel spoke of luncheon clubs, and friendship for the lonely, but Peter stressed the need to avoid being just another centre for the elderly.

May brought the conversation back to Jesus. He spent time with the poor, outcast and sick. His command to love your neighbour as yourself was a command and an invitation to follow Him. Long ago she had felt a call to be a Methodist deaconess, but she had stayed in a fairly well-paid job. Now she was retired she gave part of her time to her local Methodist church, part to community projects like this one. The church looked inwards: it was too large and cosy to want more members. There was a past history of failed church projects – coffee bars for the young; the "people next door" project twenty-five years ago. There were many good works done by individuals, but nothing from churches sponsoring local initiatives in particular areas.

Muriel also said that churchgoing did not inevitably mean people wished to be involved with others, in need or even as neighbours. Many church people saw no link between worship and the world around them. Those who did get involved answered a need in themselves, said Peter. George agreed: he was a person who was always organizing things. So too were his children. Hilda spoke of her needs after her mother had died: now she was fully involved, and the week wasn't long enough. Richard felt the worship of God must issue in action. The past divisions of the church went very deep with him: the church had much to be guilty about in this area. The Star Centre was a place where churches worked together. Muriel knew her church in the city centre had tried MSC schemes, and before that had a long

Mission Impossible?   *A Tale of Three Churches*

history of involvement in social affairs. The Star Centre was a modern equivalent of what the churches had done in the past. Richard said his neighbours had spoken of being ignored by the church when they needed help.

So the group felt strongly that many churches had failed in the past – many, though not all. Only May spoke of personal salvation as providing the reason of her own involvement in social concern. For her, there was a language of inner peace, acceptance, forgiveness. It may have been there for the others, but it was not articulated. Instead Peter spoke of a seven-days-a-week religion: the Lord requires mercy. Jesus fulfilled, not contradicted, the Old Testament Prophets and their message. This message was taken up by the vision of one clergyman, who had inspired them all. He was on the spot, rooted in the area, with great integrity. The vision was one of friendship with those who had no work of their own; often those socially ostracized; those who needed to be empowered. The Church was often the one which had failed its God. The group thus spoke of small Christian groups which worked in areas where the community spirit was far weaker than it once was. These groups would be motivated by the love of God and the example of Jesus. It would offer a sign of hope. But they would not seek to evangelize unless asked.

My reflection on these three meetings was that the old emphasis on sin and forgiveness hardly rang any bells with the group at all, bar one person. Muriel, Richard and George were all URC members, and so in the Protestant tradition, but their language was more that of moral and pastoral concern. God for them worked in all men and women; but people easily followed their self-interest in making money and their own personal issues. (Some young people provided a sharp contrast to this, however.) Christians were there to draw out the goodness in people, because of the awareness of God's love which they had found as Christians. They could offer hope for the area. The other strong element in these three people's views was that the churches so easily gave up in this task of social concern. Peter and Hilda were Anglicans. For them, too, Christianity was a matter of following Christ, of responsible stewardship, of being available. They had had a comparatively privileged life: now they wished to share their time in projects which would help others. Only May made the traditional link, in Methodist language, of God's love for sinners and the need to respond in thankful love to the needs of other people. I found this very striking. Sin as a category or concept which led to God's judgement was not a real use of language to this group.

The involvement of the local synagogue is also a factor in the development of the Star Centre. It might be thought that the co-operation between a synagogue and a church could be possible only in terms of social concern outside religious beliefs. Yet there are much deeper links than that. Here, if anywhere, is where a theology of mission might lead us in unexpected ways. The Jewish rabbi, William Wolff, became involved because of the writings of the Talmudic era from AD 100 to 500. The rabbis of that era stressed that "loving one's neighbour as yourself" (Leviticus 19:18) came in the centre of the Torah, the five books of Moses. Literally and metaphorically it was at the centre of the Torah. Throughout the holiness code of Leviticus 19 is an emphasis on help to those in need: not keeping back an employee's wages overnight (v. 13) nor leaving nothing in the fields for the poor or stranger to gather (vv. 9–10). Equally the Talmud (which quotes Jewish Halakah, or oral pronouncements on Jewish life, from rabbis who lived in the first few centuries after Jesus) speaks of a city with Jews and Gentiles, where the poor of both are fed, the sick of both are visited, both are buried, the mourners of both are comforted, and the lost goods of both are restored. There are scores of rabbinic comments on this theme. So the commentaries (Midrash) on the Psalms say that those who feed the hungry can enter the gates of the Lord (Psalm 118:20). The Hebrew word *tsedekah* is about charity, righteousness, justice, and piety. Thus the Yom Kippur (Day of Atonement) service immediately after sunset includes a mention of its charitable appeal. For the Newcastle Reform Synagogue, this included the Star Centre, in North Gosforth which was close at hand. The tradition of this synagogue, as of many others, included helping all those in need, whether or not they are Jewish.

Yet this raises profoundly what is meant by mission in terms of the relationship of synagogue and church. It was a subject raised at the 1988 Lambeth Conference by Bishop Richard Harries of Oxford, among others. For some, the evangelism of the Jews remains a high priority. For others, the common living *mitzvah* (commandment) of righteousness in Deuteronomy, Leviticus, etc. (the books of Moses) rests on Jew and Christian alike. However, they also share the same future hope of the Kingdom of God. Christians will want to affirm strongly the divinity of Jesus. Israel will look to its future Messiah, while the Church will wait for the coming of the Kingdom, which it sees inaugurated in Jesus as Messiah. So the German theologian Jürgen Moltmann argues for the common destiny of Jews and Christians.[5]

He argues that the mission to the Gentiles makes the reconciliation of the Gentiles "the last thing but one" before the final consummation of all things in the Kingdom of God. The Church is this mission of hope and its initial fulfilment through the faith of the Gentiles. It is experienced now in active mission. Yet all this only reverses the prophetic promise, which was that the Gentiles would come and worship when Zion is redeemed. Instead the Gentiles have come to praise God as the God of all creation. So what is the place of Israel in all this? Moltmann argues that the Church still is tied by the Scriptural promises to Israel. "If the church understands its origin, its historical path and its future in this way, then the church is lived hope for Israel, and Israel is lived hope for the church."

Such statements raise the most difficult questions of all for mission. Does the faithfulness of God to Israel which is the inner meaning of his promise and covenant mean anything after centuries of persecution of the Jews? What of the existence of the

Holocaust? If talk of a common destiny between Israel and the Church means anything, what does Israel mean? Israel is the rock from which the Church was hewn, to use Chris Rowland's phrase. Can it include the land and politics of Israel today? Whatever the answer to these questions, mission in Christian terms involves a hope, a spirituality and a relationship between the people of God and the world, under God. The most crucial (and unresolved) relationship is between the Church and Israel.

There is no question of any co-operation between the local church and synagogue except in terms of social concern. It is true that there is a dialogue between Christians and Jews in Newcastle (much aided by those deeply involved, such as the professor at the university, John Sawyer, who teaches Old Testament there). But the co-operation in the Star Centre is not a dialogue. It is co-operation as a sign of hope. It is worth quoting the local parish priest, Patrick Cotton, about the importance of hope in Fawdon. Writing shortly after the report *Faith in the City* was published, he spelt out the implications of the report for Fawdon, and for Christian–Jewish relations.

> The chief thrust of the report "Faith in the City" is surely to reveal the material inequality that is inherent in our society, which manifests itself in environment, health care, education as well as in prospect of future security and prosperity. We are not unfamiliar with the language of two nations, one rich one poor. With 4,000,000 unemployed this does not look like a temporary division. These facts in particular will be in the minds of those who seek to prophesy or preach, and we must surely be clear that the church should be preaching clearly and loudly at the rich and unjust. The idea of preaching is to bring Christ into the world, the church must surely present Him in the poor and persecuted.
>
> But that message is not particularly relevant to those who are impoverished. What words will time turn to truth for them? Moltmann tells the rabbinic story of a rabbi who is

seeking the answer to the question of what he will be asked on the Day of Judgement. "Have you kept the commandments?" etc. but another question came to his mind "Have you hoped for my Messiah?" Moltmann remarks Jews and Christians are peoples hoping for the Messiah.

It may be that this hoping for the Messiah is a message that will help us on. It is not a hoping for a promised land. I wonder if Judaism is now the poorer because of its possession of Jerusalem? So it is not hoping for material satisfaction here – but hoping for the Messiah – who originally chose to reveal himself in the poorest surroundings, dying the lowest of deaths. And in the richer communities, hoping for the Messiah can only come for those who are prepared, who have not avoided the fact that he may be found in the poor, and hungry, and prisoners.

Hoping for the Messiah in Fawdon

It has never been a strength of mine to envisage the Lord in fellow humans – or indeed in myself – but I do on occasions wonder, particularly when I see people going out of their way to be helpful. (Not in just simple tasks, like "I'll get your shopping if you're feeling poorly", but in the more obviously generous tasks like sitting nights with the dying, or without question, taking responsibility for Christian Aid etc.). I know that for some it is a means of self expression, but for some, it isn't that . . . Another place, I sometimes also suspect I see the finger of God is in the chronically sick who have a grasp of faith and hope, or in the old person who in serenity and graciousness, accepts their failing powers, with a seemingly undying faith.

I think I see it in a different way in the fact that, for 25 years, in unattractive surroundings, the small body of worshippers in Fawdon have laboured to make their church/hall in which they worship a holy place.

Others in Fawdon may not have the same ability to hope. If employment is improbable (if not impossible), for them the only way to come to terms is by avoiding meetings with people, and by avoiding the chance of another rejection by not applying for jobs. Apathy becomes a self defence mechanism. How can these people learn of the possibility of hope? And how should a good, unemployed Christian reveal the hope in his/her life? These questions may not be answered by me, for we must take seriously previous discussions which have consistently underlined the need to have local consultation – most particularly, each person is the only person who can reveal the hope in their lives.

The implication of Patrick Cotton's emphasis on discussions before action meant listening to other before deciding what to do. (It is the same point as in the previous section on the establishment of Shepherd's Law.) A series of well-attended local meetings led to the formation of a small group which gradually evolved into the Star Centre group. It was this group which spelt out their reasons for being involved in the discussion recorded above.

What this means for a theology of mission is an affirmation of the local community in all its richness. As Patrick Cotton said,

In the apparent despair, decay, hopelessness and unemployment in the Inner Cities, of the Urban Priority Areas, we find a richness of community that richer areas may not have. So our theology needs to set sights not merely on social justice when all are rewarded with equal finances, but on the situation which allows for the possibilities of a growth towards wholeness, in which the richness of the Inner City community life must figure significantly . . . The theology must surely try to underline the *real* richness, and underline it with confidence, for this real richness has purpose, hope and indeed presumably the stamp of divine approval – for blessed are the poor, the meek. But what is the hope and purpose?

The Star Centre is an attempt to answer that question. It is not simply by raising the area to great financial wealth that the hope will be fulfilled. Instead it must be discovered by those who live in the area themselves: "the undefinable richness found in the human interreactions of love". That can be weighed down by poverty, bad housing and unemployment. All this must be fought against. There are therefore those in the Star Centre concerned with starting their own business; those who are looking for jobs; and other such ventures. But in and through all this, there is mission as a sign of hope. Too much in the area is weighed down by apathy and an acceptance of bad schools, housing, and no consultation as a way of life.

Mission then in Fawdon means affirming people as they are, and offering a concrete sign of hope with tangible results. Moltmann has written of this hope as the essence of his theology.[6] The marks of the Church are marks of Christ establishing His Kingdom through the Church in the world: not only through the Church, but with the Church there as the one body called out to respond to God. The Church is said to be "one, holy, catholic and apostolic" in the Nicene–Constantinople Creed, dating from the Council of Constantinople in AD 381. But how is this to be understood? These terms make sense only if the Church is believed in faith to be part of God's creative activity in the Spirit. Without this they are nothing. Only if we are actively and inwardly involved with the work of God will these terms speak to us. They are statements of faith, because they speak of Christ's activity on the Church through the Spirit. Christ is one wherever He acts upon the Church, in Fawdon or in the most affluent area. The unity of the Church is the unity of believers in Christ (Galatians 3:28). It is not primarily the sociological unity of Church members. Christ gathers the Church by His activity. The holiness of the Church is the holiness of Christ who sacrifices and builds up His people: it is not initially a claim by the Church for moral superiority over others. The catholicity of the Church is the boundless Lordship of Christ, and not the fact that the Church can be found in many continents. The apostolic Church again is the mission of Christ through the Spirit to the world. The Church receives her command to go out into the world to preach the Gospel from Christ, and from Christ's apostles in the Spirit.

All this is also a statement of hope. The unity of the future salvation of the world is bound up with the unity of God's people. The Messiah will gather all people into the Kingdom – old and young, rich and poor, black and white. There will be one Kingdom. The holiness of this Kingdom is that it will reflect the glory of God, which will fill the earth. The Church is holy because it anticipates this new creation: in hope it reflects this glory. The apostolate of the Church belongs to the beginning of the new age: in its very activity of mission it is a sign of hope for the world. Finally to the extent that the Church is open to the coming unity of this Kingdom, the Church is catholic.

For one small activity in one suburb these are large, not to say enormous claims. But they are the claims given to the Church by Christ. They are not signs of merit or moral superiority. They exist insofar as the Church is open to the Spirit's work.

Peter's comment in the group about Christian motivation being, he hoped, attractive to others even if it is not always seen as "religious" is echoed in Moltmann's concept of Christian holiness being a sign of hope at the dawning glory of God in creation which shines out in power. May's comment about the Church too often looking inwards highlights the difficulty the Church finds in expressing a catholicity: for the Church in turning in on itself turns away from the coming unity of the Kingdom. The group was certainly aware of the complicity of the world and the Church in the suffering of Christ; but mission for them was not averting the wrath of God on others. Instead it was an awareness of the love of God for them which motivated them.

So in an impoverished area, they sought to offer hope by drawing out the goodness of others.

Ascension Outreach Project, North Kenton

> Why should we talk of urban spirituality at all? Surely wherever we are we still need to pray and to read our Bibles and to worship with the church?
> Of course in many ways what we do as Christians in an urban environment is fundamentally the same as it would be anywhere else on this planet. Yet what differs is the setting in which the individual Christian pursues his devotion. The culture in which he lives and the pressures which impinge upon him will lead to different attitudes to God and His world according to the milieu in which he lives.
> It is a sad fact that we are still two nations and often we have no idea of the pressures under which our brothers and sisters are living out their lives. Of course not all is difficult and there are very special joys to be discovered in places like the inner city or council housing estate. The joys are frequently intense in a way that is not often true of the affluent areas or the suburbs. Nevertheless the pain of the urban situation is something which has to be experienced to be fully understood.[7]

> Christians in UPAs [Urban Priority Areas – the inner cities and outer council estates] are seeking community. Where they survive, it is because they have found it in some form. Their theologies reflect different visions of community, different ways to it but all are best analysed as theologies of community ... They are developed by people who, unable to live without community, find from experience that the earthly city cannot provide it ... They experience the city as injustice, impotence and loneliness. So they seek another city "with foundations"

and see its rallying point in the Church.[8]

Both these writers underline the difficulty of urban spirituality. Therefore any project, any mission of the Church in an area beset by deprivation, must recognize the difficulties of the outer estate. These are very different from those of the suburban or rural parish. It is doubtful whether each area really appreciates the problems of the other. Thus the Ascension Outreach Project would never have been easy. It finally ended after I left the area, and the reasons involved in the ending are not my concern. What is interesting is how this project, which is not far from the Star Centre at Fawdon but which took place on a very deprived estate, managed to put down roots in the area, and drew local people into some form of Christian worship and community.

In 1982 the parish of The Ascension, Kenton, Newcastle, began to plan a new project, which later came to be called "Ascension Outreach". It centred on one estate, of about 10,000 people, known as the North Kenton Estate. Few people came to church from there, and the estate was primarily made up of local authority housing. It had many social problems of unemployment and deprivation. In 1984 the parish entered an agreement with the Diocese of Newcastle, the Newcastle City Deanery and the Church Army. With the material support of all four bodies, the parish priest, the Rev. John Dewar, began work on the estate with two Church Army sisters. Their brief was to live on the estate, and to work there for three years. Their job description gives an aim and an objective: "to show the people of North Kenton their need of our Saviour Jesus Christ" (aim) and "to establish a residential Christian presence on the North Kenton Estate" (objective). Six duties were also mentioned (given in abbreviated form here).

1. To use the Community Office.
2. Religious instruction and youth involvement.
3. To aid local residents in need.

4. To maintain a presence at all times.
5. To work with single people.
6. To further the work of the Church.

There had been for some years a parish church off the estate, in a slightly more prosperous area. Between the two lay a busy road. Few on the North Kenton Estate worshipped at the parish church, and the estate had a reputation for being impossible territory for all save the Roman Catholics. Only the "occasional offices" related estate and parish church. The time came when there was no curate at the parish church. After some years, the Ascension Outreach Project began.

The job description speaks of "developing contacts with the residents". There was a great deal of alienation and anomie on the estate. Family breakups, single parents, loneliness and unresolved tensions were common. A quarter of young mothers were estimated by one professional worker on the estate to have been in care. The pattern of some young people's development was familiar: school truancy, dole, avoiding the MSC, loose cohabitation and children. Ten years ago many families were rehoused on the estate from other parts of Newcastle. Few mothers were married, and many of them had had their first child by the age of nineteen. Domestic violence was common, and vandalism by young people was also frequent. Having said that, there were many good and caring people on the estate and there were times of joy as well as suffering.

The local authority had responded by many initiatives, including moving housing offices to be located on the estate for easy access; toddler groups; the Block Project which provides accommodation for local groups; and the Priority Area Team. The Church Army sisters had not sought to duplicate this work. Instead they had got to know people, befriended them, helped them to get in touch with local authority officers and often became deeply involved in many families. This had been a costly, emotionally demanding role, offering much enjoyment but also a constant degree of stress. It had not been simply presenting an example for local people to imitate. The Singles Club was a formal expression of many relationships formed in the estate.

The project had a basic commitment to evangelism. It was there in the job description ("to show the people of North Kenton their need of our Saviour Jesus Christ . . .") and it was there in the sisters' own understanding of the project. However, it was not a view of Christ as absent from the estate. Rather they saw the Holy Spirit as active both in the lives of those who lived there and in the initiatives of the local authority and voluntary agencies. The aim of the sisters was to draw out from local people some understanding of this divine activity, and to relate it to the Incarnation.

Thus they involved themselves in local worship, baptism and funeral visits and Sunday clubs. This was related to the parish church in varying degrees. Baptism and funeral visits involved the parish church directly. Some local worship relied on the support of the church youth group for music, drama etc. Finally, Bible studies in one of the flats with a few local people were quite independent of the parish church, although some went on to confirmation preparation.

Why does it matter what the relationship was with the parish church? Mainly because the Church in any institutional form was seen as alien to the estate, since the Methodists pulled out after their church was burnt down; the Roman Catholics were seen as self-contained and concerned with money; and the Church of England vicar was seen as living in a different area. The church was a failure, and any attempt at evangelism would be in the middle, a punchball between church and estate.

Nevertheless, worship was successful on the estate. At Christmas and Easter in both years a play drew in twenty-five estate children as actors, and sixty in the audience, with hymns and prayers interwoven with it. There were several small Bible groups and a confirmation course, and about eight people went to the parish church from the estate. Part of this work was hindered by a shortage of funds to buy even hymn books for the estate. Family services were started on particular occasions such as Easter, the July Festival and Harvest. Over thirty attended these services in the Block and the sisters were able to further develop these to become regular monthly family services.

The strategy was that of evangelism, a Christian presence and some community work. It emerged slowly, as an attempt not to duplicate already existing work. Leadership was given in some projects (the float at the Festival, the Block, Singles Club, summer trips) but the aim was to encourage local initiative. It was work which attempts to break the feeling of hopelessness, apathy and being on the receiving end of organized care. It was only a small-scale parable, but nevertheless fragmented activities were and are a parable of escape from vicious circles. The vicious circle was that whatever the rehousing, the new resources of social work care, the improvement schemes, the area was seen as always "demanding" more, and not responding but remaining dependent. In the words of J. Moltmann, in *The Crucified God*:

> Though hardly anyone today believes in a personal devil, many people speak, in a variety of spheres of life, of vicious circles, of the vicious circles of poverty, of violence, of alienation, of industrial pollution, of the vicious circles of the black, the prisoner, the immigrant worker and the mentally ill. What does it mean?

North Kenton was full of such circles: violence, pollution, single parents, unemployment and so on. What matters is Moltmann's answer, for it is the answer of the project, and the demonstration of a strategy. The project was a symbol of identification with suffering in sensitivity, love and hope for the future. The parabolic nature of the Incarnation speaks of new life, and openness to the future, through acts of healing, preaching and worship. So too did this project.

What was essential was the overall aim building up of community as a whole; worship and the nurture of Christian community as a sign of hope; community work which was directly related to the encouragement of human dignity and life-giving personal relationships. In brief, it was of the nature of the project to be fragmented in its activities yet clear in its aim: identification with the history of the crucified and risen Christ, whose history broke the vicious circle. When he was reviled, he did not retaliate ... The theological understanding was not incidental but essential.

The project was always clear that it was not simply increasing the congregation of The Ascension, North Kenton, and that the estate had deep-seated problems of unemployment, housing and community identity. But there was a clash between the parish church and the project. The policy on baptisms did cause tension – it would never have been easy to implement any policy, given the geographical and sociological distinctions between the area around the parish church, where most of the worshipping congregation lived, and the deprived nature of the estate. In any case, the church is up a hill from the estate; there are no buses on a Sunday morning and few have cars; it is a long way to push a pram for a 9.30 a.m. baptismal service. But the other side of the policy must be stated. The parish priest felt that it was one thing to offer love and compassion to an estate: this was a theology of creation, of presence, of divine identification. It was something else to respond to Christ as a baptized follower. Such commitment demanded attendance at church by the parents of a child to be baptized, or by the adult; demanded baptism during the main Eucharist; and was a costly process. There appeared to be a tension between a desire to reveal God's love by living on the estate, and a calling out from the world in baptism.

It was not that the two policies cannot be reconciled, but that to do so required an understanding of why sacramental grace in baptism was guarded with such care. If a Christian community were to emerge around the family worship every month, might not baptism be celebrated there as well? The same argument also applies to funerals. Against this was the need to maintain links between the parish church and the estate.

The story of the Ascension Project is about mission by listening to local people on the estate; developing a relationship with them and a spirituality appropriate to the estate; and only then beginning to act in the area alongside local people and not for them. Such a policy is bound to lead to tensions with the existing church. At the same time the project was deeply involved in the community. It placed the sisters in the self-help groups, community service, credit unions and community centres. There was a never-ending stream of demands and requests. Work with young children, summer outings, helping people in debt – the demands of such an area are enormous.

But so too are the rewards. When the Estate Festival went well, and a corporate group was formed for monthly worship, there was a sense of great achievement. "The greatest barrier to a healthy spirituality in the inner city is an endemic sense of failure", writes John Pearce. He notices the sense of being at the bottom of the heap and being rejected. Thus one of the main problems for the project was whether it could exist on its own terms; when the project did work well, there was a sense of having accomplished something against enormous odds.

Laurie Green's book *Power to the Powerless* is a study of a similar project in a working-class parish in Birmingham which ran for many years. It is interesting that his book in the end turns on what power and powerlessness means for people in this situation. He examines the many forms of power, such as physical, political, economic, cultural and spiritual power. He asks whether good can win in such an experience, turning to the trials and crucifixion of Jesus. After showing how the structures of society do often prevent attempts to change and improve local communities, Laurie Green described how a Bible group in his church had discovered the centrality of the death of Jesus to their local situation.[9]

Jesus' death on the cross is no pathetic submission to or acceptance of death's authority either but a sinewy test of love. The cross demonstrates, firstly, his total solidarity with those who are oppressed by evil, secondly, it placards and displays evil's ugliness back to the world. Thirdly, through the cross Jesus makes God's ultimate protest through evil; and finally and profoundly, it brings the key to unlock history. These four elements could only be achieved by the powerful powerlessness of the cross. It seems folly to the worldly wise until they are asked how to defeat evil in any other way than by displaying the integrity of love.

Power and powerlessness are what the Ascension Project was concerned with. Whether the small discoveries of relationships, friendships, worship and community action will flourish remains to be seen. This is not a false or sentimental optimism. It is instead witnessing to a peace which is possible in the midst of disillusionment and the disintegration of many plans. It is not a peace which retreats from society into quietism and inactivity, but one that accepts the strength born of inner spiritual conviction that can resist the manipulations of others in greater power.[10]

Conclusion

This chapter has sought to think about three local situations in a way which is honest and also theological. It has used the comments of local people and clergy and tried to describe how it seemed both to them and to myself at the time. It began at St Mary's, Monkseaton, by thinking about the corporate priesthood of the Church alongside the nature of dependence and the freeing of ourselves from a false security.

I could not help feeling that I was in the presence of something as important and significant for the "Kingdom of God" as all the busy schemes and strategies that I was currently involved in or knew of... We were faced continually with the mystery of the Trinity and our own pride and frailty.[11]

Then at the Star Centre the issue remains still the way the Church is involved in the area as a sign of the Kingdom. How that often over-used phrase is thought through and acted on becomes crucial in Fawdon. It involves a consideration of relationships with the local synagogue; of the nature of hope; of the nature of the Church. Finally there is the attempt both to evangelize and to engage in community work in North Kenton. Here the issue is not simply one of hope. It involves far more the question of what power and powerlessness actually mean in practice. There is too the recurrent nature of the failure of initiatives on this estate. It is not all hopeless, but the Church does not escape the problems simply by appealing to some transcendent "God up there".

Powerlessness; hope; shared ministry. Are these issues for mission? Certainly each example cited above involved a relationship with God, and learning to find the significance of our loves. Equally each example described particular pieces of action, in response to what was seen as local needs. Each example is not an enormous success. But then the Christian story is about sharing with others the possibility of trust, forgiveness and being recognized by God, Who is always ahead of us and before us. That does not involve a community whose only basis is success and achievement. It is time to look more closely at how mission might be defined.

CHAPTER 2

What is Mission?

Faces along the bar
Cling to their average day:
The lights must never go out,
The music must always play,
All the conventions conspire
To make this fort assume
The furniture of home;
Lest we should see where we are,
Lost in a haunted wood,
Children afraid of the night
Who have never been happy or good.

W. H. Auden, "September, 1939"

What are days for?
Days are where we live.
They come, and they wake us
Time and time over.
They are to be happy in:
Where can we live but days?
Ah, solving that question
Brings the priest and the doctor
In their long coats
Running over the fields.

Philip Larkin, "Days"

In the spring of 1987 I was part of a group which was invited to look at the Sunderland South Circuit of the Methodist Church.

Sunderland was once a rich town, building ships for the world: in those days Methodism had a strong presence in the town, with many local benefactors. Today it suffers from high unemployment, and while some churches flourish, others hang on and hope for better times. The churches we visited had spent much time looking honestly at their future, gathering comments from all sides. Some of the feelings expressed were typical.

> Preponderance of elderly; not enough people able to take responsibility for offices so that these can be shared round and changes of personnel made; constant repairs needed on the beautiful, oldfashioned, large church; declining membership; older people are willing on the whole to "suffer" change.

> Since Mission England there has been a period of some growth with new members and teachers emerging. Others have joined the church family too. However, currently I notice a falling away. There are some very faithful and dependable people who have been here for some time as well as some new dedicated Christians. The faithful are mainly elderly although there are a few between 20 and 40 years of age. The problem is one of inconsistency which makes the continuity of the work difficult from time to time . . . We cannot protect the grounds. As soon as fencing is repaired it is demolished.

> On arrival in September 1983 I was told by a number of people that the church should have closed ten years ago. It has held on and continues to do so. There is a will to survive for the future . . . "hang on and hope for better days!"

Further examples could be given, but the point is made. There are other churches in the circuit which are growing ("a good mixed age group . . . a real interest in opening up church for service to community . . . a quiet air of optimism with a good family atmosphere"). No congregation, however, found growth easy, and their involvement with the community, while strong, tended to reflect the pattern of an earlier age. Indeed, membership had declined from almost 2,000 to 1,000 in the twelve years up to 1987. Furthermore the circuit was strongest in the suburban areas, and weakest in the large council estates. So as the town declined, and young people moved away with relatively few coming in, the church declined with it. It is not a crisis, nor is it unmitigated gloom; there are churches with new policies and changing worship; but it remains true that the crucial factor is that of survival. Similar stories could probably be told of the other denominations. Why is this? Why, in spite of changes and experiments, is the overall picture one of a high degree of tradition and slow decline? We need to look more carefully at what mission is.

Secularization

Brian Wilson has argued that in the United Kingdom churches and religious belief are losing their social significance. The mainstream religions gradually lose their importance, and fall off in numbers. A few small religious groups do flourish by offering comfort to those without any hope; the irrationality of their faith is persuasive for those whom life appears to offer precisely nothing. But in the majority of the modern world religion declines. Brian Wilson views this process with dismay, but with resignation as being inevitable. Religion can no longer celebrate local life, nor can it support a morality of love, trust and loyalty which in turn undergirds the social order. "Modern society rejects religion on intellectual grounds and fails to see what the cost might be in terms of the emotional sustenance that men need in order to live."[1]

His argument has been very controversial. His chief critics are two Anglican sociologists, David Martin (who now works primarily in America) and Robin Gill. What reasons do Gill and

Martin give for rejecting Wilson's view of religion in society? The argument for a secular society is that religion is in decline; it conforms more and more to the world; the world is seen less and less as sacred and able to be explained in rational terms only; society disengages itself from religion, and therefore religion becomes more and more inward, making no appearance outside the area of the religious group; and society itself carries out the rituals and patterns of behaviour provided once by religion.[2]

David Martin gives a less clear-cut answer to why churchgoing has declined in Britain. All voluntary associations have declined in Britain this century, whether religious or secular. Churches may have survived these changes better than most. Religion has become a private affair in modern societies, and belief reflects many different reasons for commitment to a religion. Christianity is in a partial recession, notes Martin (though it must be noted, eleven years on from Martin's essay, that the resurgence of Christianity in its extreme Protestant form seems assured). It is decreasingly used to provide the official justification of the State. The pagan or magical element in the Christian religion has revived. He sees Christianity in the modern industrial world, from the Soviet Union to Somerset, from Poland to Pennsylvania, as facing indifference; magic; nationalism; liberalism; scientism; and Marxism. It is a powerful group to be in conflict with. But, of course, there frequently is not conflict, but collusion and compromise. Christian support for nationalism in Eastern Europe is well known. However, it is liberalism which makes religious practice most difficult. Nationalism is based on particular languages and groups of people: in this sense, the North-East of England often feels like a religion with its own fierce nationalism. Certainly the churches have seen the defence of a regional identity as an important issue for them, and the theme of a North-East identity will recur throughout this book. Over against nationalism stands liberalism, or a cosmopolitan way of life. Clearly liberalism can be defined in many ways, and frequenty has been a target of theologians. Here it is taken in a sociological and geographical sense: the rebuilding of the cities since the Second World War, with planned council estates and private developments, was a significant improvement on what went before. But within these cities there is a way of life which Martin describes well: it "corrodes the sense of locality and local loyalty, undermines dialect speech and minority languages and espouses a functional morality hostile to irrational taboo and suprarational sanctity." However, it is also true that local dialect still flourishes, and the cults of spooks, Ouija boards and other aspects of the occult are still common on many estates. Nevertheless the general impression is correct. Martin continues, "This mentality is mobile, shifting, hedonistic"; it is interested in how things work, with little sense of personal guilt.[3] There is however an enlarged sense of collective guilt, so that institutions and cultures are easily blamed and held responsible. Again this is a familiar pattern: the frequently expressed dissatisfaction with the local council may well be justified, but it is also the only form of guilt and blame clearly recognized in a pleasure-seeking society. Other aspects of personal responsibility are less easily articulated, for the basis of society is satisfactory performance. Abstract concepts like citizenship or rights (however much politicians attempt to evoke the notion of the good or active citizen) ring hollow in most people's ears. Thus we live in an urbanized society with "its symbols dirtied by poor moral performance relative to expectation, its myths downgraded by criticism", and we see the decline of churchgoing.[4]

Yet it is not as straightforward as this account implies, and Martin realizes this. All across Europe there is provincial resentment at national rule from the centre. The Basques in Spain, Britanny in France, parts of Scandinavia, and of course Wales, Scotland, Northern England and Northern Ireland reject what they see as loss of power and influence. Alienation from the centre gives power to minority religious groups. Language, religion and way of life thus support each other against what is, often correctly, seen as dominance by another part of the country. Thus the growth of small Protestant groups, sometimes as a part of the house-church movement, reflects the assertion of regional identity and way of life.

Thus we see two cultures which are in tension. One is mobile, transitory, shifting and hedonistic. This Martin calls the "liberal culture". It is not strongly devoted to consumption, but it is increasingly marked by the products of the mass culture in which we live, especially by the mass media. The other is local or regional, and defends an older way of life. Where this culture takes a religious form it will often be puritanical (such as an anti-pornography movement) and have clear stereotypes of male and female behaviour. Between the two there is a struggle between the identity of people expressed in their language and their myths, and the ever-growing world of rational explanations and of technology. The power of regional or local collective identity has been a dominant force in North-East England for decades: indeed much of Nonconformist religion allied itself with local political campaigns, and it became impossible to say whether a particular action was motivated by religion, politics or regional identity. As the region becomes less and less powerful in the nation, so the strains in the North-East become more acute. So too the tension within the region between an older way of life and the brash, new culture becomes acute, as many recent commentators have noticed. The brash culture of the vast Metro Centre shopping development at Gateshead is the symbol of "liberal culture" in the region. It is now the largest shopping centre in Europe.

There are other features of our secular society which should be noted. I have already mentioned the interest in magic, astrology and even witchcraft. Although this is seldom expressed openly, there is a widespread fatalism combined with pseudo-scientific explanations. Another reaction to widespread anonymity is that of mysticism, where the traditional understanding in Christianity of God as personal becomes changed into a superhuman force, found in nature and experiences of life as out-of-the-ordinary. Then there are political expressions of religious belief, where myths relating to long-held political values and ideas are taken quite literally. Liberty, fraternity, equality and democracy become the driving force behind movements which give complete meaning to people's lives. Where once people would have worshipped some form of the Christian God, however much allied with magical or pagan beliefs, political messianism now takes their place. The Militant movement, or some local political crusade, appeals to an idealism which religion once met. In a more ugly vein, nationalism and racism combine with political idealism to produce a powerful National Front movement among the young unemployed – especially for a while in the former steel town of Consett.[5] These irrational forces flourish because on the one hand the affluence of much of modern society is not available for young people who face a choice between dead-end jobs and government training schemes; on the other, the instability of modern liberalism lies in its emptiness of rhetoric and its inability to provide any place for ceremony, historical myth and a sense of the sacred. In an affluent society, such ancient values may be let go into a private religion combined with a vague civic duty. In the less affluent, peripheral society of the regions, especially in once-proud areas such as the North-East, the irrational powers of cults and beliefs become a strong alternative.

Finally, there is the return of the so-called "Victorian values", much associated with some members of the present government. The point here is that in a secular society where religion no longer easily undergirds social norms, and where there is a need for greater economic efficiency, it is not surprising that politicians should take over the language of religion, and preach the need for a "Protestant ethic" of hard work, personal self-discipline and conformity. The system produces conformity by internal assent: there is less need for direct control, except where crime and vandalism occurs. It is striking that David Martin in an article in 1976 predicted a partial return of political appeals for a stress on duty, discipline and reliability.[6] Again the issue is not party-political: it is how a society holds together in a private, individual and pluralist world. For some political leaders the answer will be an intense dissatisfaction with what they call "liberal Christianity" and an attack on its official leaders for a more clear-cut religion which serves the needs of a technical society. The only problem, but it is a fatal one, is that those most interested in promoting technology cannot also carry themselves the role of religious leadership – although the mass media will attempt that substitution as well, producing a national leadership both interested in technology and with heavy religious overtones. This is precisely what "Thatcherism" means for many people.

For many people, however, and perhaps the majority, none of this still describes where they are. Indifferent to political appeals for Victorian values; repelled by the dogmatism of political cults and movements, and by the interest in the occult; no longer attracted by the older culture in their region, nor by those religious groups which associate themselves with it; long since lapsed from regular practice inside a religious denomination, and equally disinterested in a private mysticism; their own place, it would seem, lies within the technical, rational world of mass culture, with its horizons bounded by greater consumption, knowledge and personal relationships. Certainly this world offers far more personal freedom to most people than the past ever did. It is not as though the churches should reject this new way of life, though many in the churches do oppose modern civilization and mass culture, fearful of what they bring. There is inside and outside the churches enormous interest in personal issues such as AIDS, feminism, children's rights, gay power and the like. It is the way which Don Cupitt feels the new Christian ethic will go: sensitive to self-expression, authenticity and self-awareness.[7] But for others there is still an appeal to some invisible religion. Children are christened as an unexpressed assumption of everyday life, as John Habgood puts it. Religion allows a sense of belonging, and belief in an ultimate meaning to life. The sense of belonging is more diffuse than a commitment to regional nationalism, but it is just as powerful. Many people feel that the clergy look down on these half-articulated beliefs. Yet it is for them a sign of the way the world is, bound up with notions of fate, danger and protection against harm. It is a religion of privacy, with a desire to create one's own sense of significance, individual value and worth. Belief is not simply personal or subjective, but private: it is withdrawal into a private world, where my belief is an expression of my opinion.

Therefore, we cannot simply chart a secular society by measuring churchgoing. Quite apart from the vexed question of how religious the medieval peasant was anyway, there are many forms of expressing religious belief in the contemporary world. It cannot be the case that religious belief is equated with commitment to religious institutions, such as churches. Stephen Yeo's classic study of Reading before 1914 showed just how damaging to all voluntary groups was the growth of modern civilization, with its mass organization of leisure, employment and eventually welfare. Mary Douglas has argued that close-knit primitive societies have strong ritual expressions of religion: much looser primitive societies are much less ordered in their religious life. We live in a society with a strong split between the public and the private life.

Life then for those in the last decades of the twentieth century is an uneasy blending of the older religious beliefs in significance and protection, and the enormous possibility of personal freedom, which may or may not satisfy us. We can choose between the very beliefs which can give meaning to our lives. If we choose to reject any belief, we are free to investigate with intense introversion how we feel about our personal relationships in such a universe. All that there is is our own autonomy. We are condemned to freedom, whether we like it or not. We must choose our own morality.

Wilson's argument that religion is losing its social significance may then be true, but it is not the issue for local churches. Instead of a slow but steady intellectual rejection of Providence which results in agnosticism or atheism, there is an enormous variety of religious beliefs, some public, some private. This interacts with questions of regional and national identity; with degrees of affluence and urbanization; with political movements and appeals for greater civic duty; and with a desire to celebrate, in however obscurely articulated a manner, the moments of significance in a person's life. Beyond all this is the relentless stress on personal freedom and authenticity.

In the face of this enormous pluralism and variety, discussing the mission of the Church may seem like pressing the accelerator when the car is stuck in the snow. There will be much noise, the wheels will spin faster and faster, but nothing much will happen. At worst one will only sink deeper into the snowdrift. Yet if one simply accepts an analysis of society as post-religious, which in effect is what most writers about Britain today actually settle for, then Christianity becomes tentative, a cultural gloss and a debating chamber. Alternatively, as the Jewish novelist Chaim Bermant spoke of his own faith, religious practice becomes an "antique of the mind": it is cultivated as some enjoy food or wine, or appreciated as foreign travel is appreciated – a change from the everyday. For those who follow the path of liberal Christianity, this system of belief may or may not be true but it provides great consolation of existence: a way of coping with the dying child, by means of the forgotten story of a dying man. In a less tragic vein, it can also provide celebration and private hope, which can give greater meaning to what we have in fact achieved for ourselves. But such a private faith, meeting the existential crises of life, is vulnerable to further divisions into what is significant for women, for ethnic minorities, for one's own private story.

In short there is no public dimension to this faith.[8] The promise of forgiveness, liberation and new life must be taken up again. It is perhaps a little clearer why it is difficult for churches to flourish, whether in Sunderland or anywhere else. But it is no nearer to laying the groundwork for mission – unless clearing the ground helps in that task. It is time to turn back to the origins of Christianity, not to escape from the modern world, but in order that the nature of Christianity may be seen as an illumination of our present existence. Mission cannot be an answer to the needs of the modern world, for Christians are as much part of its needs and problems as anyone: but the Christian Gospel may shed some light on the path to a more complete existence, as Augustine felt in Carthage centuries ago:

> the difference . . . between those who see the goal that they must reach, but cannot see the road by which they are to reach it, and those who see the road to that blessed country which is meant to be no mere vision but our home.[9]

The New Testament Church

In recent years much attention has been paid to the crisis which gripped Judaism at the time of Jesus. Thus, such books as John Riches's *Jesus and the Transformation of Judaism*, or Christopher Rowland's *Christian Origins*, with its subtitle "An Account of the Setting and Character of the Most Important Messianic Sect of Judaism", show that the ministry of Jesus cannot be seen except in the context of God's agreement with Israel. Rowland's book ends with two evocative titles for the concluding sections: "The Separation of Church and Synagogue" and "You are his Disciples but we are Disciples of Moses".

Jesus' ministry to Judaism was about His preaching of the Kingdom, which itself refers to the relationship of God to His people. All His teaching and actions concerned the vision of God Who would not destroy his enemies and rewarded those who remained faithful to Him. John the Baptist clung to the notion of a destructive God coming in judgemental power, although he broke away from the Jewish way of thinking. But for Jesus the "holy war" to which people are called involved love and prayer. It was an invitation to join a community which was responding to the Kingdom and was centred on the idea of affecting existence in an unconventional way.

Such an invitation went against current ideas of God. For other religious groups at the time, such as the Qmram community or the Zealots, the world was in the grip of evil and alien powers. These could be seen as Caesar, Satan, or other foreign rulers. If this sharp division is made between the rule of God and evil, then God can only rule when the forces of evil have been overthrown, and destroyed. That is why the Zealot community advocated leaving home and family to prepare for a long struggle as God's soldiers against the occupying power. The idea of soldiers for God has a long tradition in Christianity, but the ministry of Jesus did not embrace it – whatever we may think while singing "Onward Christian Soldiers". Equally the Qmram community envisaged a heavenly welfare between the armies of Satan and the armies of the covenant (as in their documents, the *War Rule* and the *Community Rule*). This small community claimed to have the authority to renew Judaism, guided by their own Teacher of Righteousness. They saw themselves as children of light, profoundly grateful for the mercy of God, in a way similar to Paul's understanding of justification (or righteousness) by faith alone. Such a community breathed "a fanatical conviction that, however much the odds may have been stacked against them, the legions of angels would come to the aid of the righteous, as they struggled with the forces of darkness."[10] They were strongly hostile to the leaders of the Jerusalem Temple as wicked priests. Their end was probably destruction by the Roman army, perhaps as they prepared themselves for the final, heavenly battle.

So there were alternatives to the way Jesus behaved (and the Sadducees, Scribes and Pharisees could also be mentioned). But Jesus struggled with the power of evil by prayer: His healing miracles demonstrate that the evil in the world, which Jesus certainly recognized and judged, would be overcome by healing and forgiveness. God is not a God of battles, but a Father who forgives His children. The power of God is found in the midst of healing and forgiveness. "Love your enemies and pray for those who persecute you, so that you may be sons of your Father who is in heaven."

Therefore, Jesus addresses the experience of the people of Israel. The long struggle of the Jewish nation becomes the basis for a new understanding of the nature of God. Their own experiences of poverty and loss become focused in meals of salvation and rejoicing. The religious (or cultic) meal was once a means by which the people of Israel took part in the power of God, with a communal sacrifice. After the exile the priestly offerings for sin and guilt become dominant, while the Passover meal looked back to the deliverance of Israel and forward to the future Kingdom. Jesus' meals were not tied to particular times and cults, but were spontaneous. They stressed the power of salvation in the present, with an understanding of forgiveness and fulfilment.

Jesus called people to take their experiences of loss, hunger, poverty and rejection into meals of fellowship and reconciliation. In all of this the understanding of the nature of God is at stake. It is more than simply an extension of loving one's neighbour. It is an invitation to understand love as present most when relationships are disordered, vengeance and hatred are accepted, and people are rejected. The answer to this is a transformation of human existence by the presence of God's power. But the reason for believing in this possibility was Jesus' portrayal of God as a greater reality than the forces of evil and separation.

Jesus never explained the phrase "Kingdom of God". He assumed that His hearers would have taken the phrase as familiar or even self-evident. In the translations (Targums) of the biblical Hebrew into the everyday Aramaic language of Jesus, the Kingdom of God was simply a way of speaking of God reigning. It is an image which describes the presence of God in the everyday world. But the image was not a concept to be analysed. It caught the imagination, as Jesus' parables and actions did as well. There were many who failed to understand: Mark 3:22–30 shows clearly that some Jewish hearers of Jesus only had their suspicions of Him as an envoy of Satan confirmed when He healed.[11]

The Kingdom, then, is not a social club nor a business venture. It does not decline or grow, whatever the secularization of society. We do not build the Kingdom. That is one of the oldest Protestant myths that there is. As the introduction to this book stressed (p. 0), seeing the Kingdom is a matter of imagination and vision. Yet it is not a fictitious entity. God's rule was active in the ministry of Jesus, though it was yet to come in its full reality. Jesus understood His ministry as an expression of that divine rule over humanity. It was important that there was a response to it. It was not a concept to be debated, nor was it simply an expression of meaning in the life of an individual. It is for these reasons that liberal Christianity (in the sense of being a cultural phenomenon, which is a matter of private opinion) cannot be accepted as compatible with the teaching of Jesus.

The Kingdom evokes a response. The response may be individual, as in the forgiveness of one person by another – graphically illustrated in the parable of the king who forgives a huge debt, but is angry with those who will not forgive others. But the response can also be communal, including the concern for all those who are poor and disadvantaged (Matthew 25:31–46). In all this there is the challenging and reversal of accepted values – unexpected possibilities and realities in negative situations. The final constraint on Jesus was that of the death to which He was sentenced. The fact that the Jewish authorities were willing to hand Jesus over to a Roman court shows the seriousness of the situation. It is likely that Jesus was interrogated by the Jewish authorities, and seriously threatened their security by his implicit claims to absolute authority. Jesus' death is not simply a symbol of self-giving love. The death of Jesus is on behalf of the world, and the Gentile centurion in Mark is a sign of those many who will recognize the death as an act of salvation for the world.

Did Jesus call his followers to co-operate in this overcoming of evil and darkness? The early Church would have shaped the material about the call of Jesus (and so itself contributed to the New Testament writings on mission), but it seems to be the case that Jesus recast the doctrine of rewards and punishment by God into an understanding of God's relationship with His whole creation, which is one of seeking their ultimate good ("blessing those who curse you"). To follow Jesus meant to be committed to a vision of the mercy and love of God. Perhaps Jesus expected the end to come with the response of the people of Israel to His ministry. However, Jesus also called some to go out and preach, healing and demonstrating the coming of the Kingdom. Parts of the gospels show an attitude of watching and waiting in the hope of a final end of history. Equally, Jesus may not have been concerned with the issue of when the end would come: rather He wanted to focus on the love and mercy of God, which He exemplified on the cross by his death "as a ransom for many".

The implication for an understanding of mission is enormous. The response to the Resurrection was the establishment of a community which rejected the separation of the people of God from the world. Whatever may be the social significance of the churches, the nature of mission is clear:

> Jesus is evidently present in the community ... He is present where the community gathers in faith (Matthew 18:20) and will remain with the community as it begins its mission in the world (28:20). He is the exalted Son of Man to whom all authority has been given (28:16). The entire Gospel story is a proclamation of this abiding presence. The miracle stories affirm that the risen Jesus continues to effect healing, liberation and forgiveness within the community ... The Lord is also present in the community's mission. The call to the Twelve remains the marching orders for Matthew's own

community (10:11). The rebuffs and persecutions the missionaries experience are a share in Jesus's own ministry and experience (10:24). This same abiding Lord and glorified Son of Man is the one who sends the community out on mission at the end of the Gospel and promises to remain with the missionary church (28:16–20).[12]

What is crucial in the world of the first century is the teaching of Jesus, which remains open to society, but does not simply become a social activity. Instead His life reveals the presence of the eternal God in time. Jesus is God's love occurring in our time and history. In His ministry our lives are restored to an authentic way of existence. It is not simply a moral act of titanic human striving. In the story told of Jesus, the activity of God is present. Therefore, mission for the Church is that activity which follows the life of Jesus, so that forgiveness and reconciliation become a reality. The implication for the Church is that there is an openness to society; preaching the good news of the Kingdom for the whole of creation and seeking a communal and personal response to that good news, which will lead into joining in God's own mission to the world. We turn finally in this chapter to the question of boundaries.

The Local Church and Mission

So far we have looked at one typical group of churches in Sunderland. The explanation for their decline lies in the gradual permeation of our whole culture with a belief that religion is mere opinion, and of private concern only. It is not that we are necessarily a less religious country, for Wilson is wrong to link religious behaviour to churchgoing. There are many forms of expressing religious feelings and beliefs, as our survey showed. Yet in all of this diversity, churches themselves become less and less important. Religion is seen as "really" the vehicle of group identity, or it is felt that baptisms, weddings and funerals (the rites of passage) are the result of group pressure.[13]

No doubt much of this is true, and theologians should not ignore the considerable insights of sociologists. But an attempt to articulate what mission is, or might be, cannot simply return to the explanations of folk religion as the vestiges of an earlier culture. In a society where the most significant turning-point for many young people is acquiring a mortgage, and the sense of identity as a house-owner is what one must struggle to maintain by keeping up the mortgage payments, the older forms of communal identity and personal significance may be very weak indeed.[14] Anthony Archer's fine study of the Catholic Church in Newcastle-on-Tyne shows how much the sense of a Catholic, Irish identity has weakened throughout this century. Once there was a strong, working-class, urban culture in which the priest and the social and devotional life of the Church played a strong part. Again good sociological reasons could be given. Today, while a much greater sense of identity persists among Catholics than in other denominations, the emphasis falls on private faith, and individual response to God. In the Catholic Church in the North-East, as elsewhere, the strength of this is greater commitment and a far more thought-out faith. I once met an elderly lady who had become a Catholic in her late teens before the Second World War, much to the intense anger of her parents. When she was received into the Catholic Church, the nun who had instructed her asked her what present she would like. She asked for a (Catholic) Bible. The answer was met with disbelief and incomprehension, and some while later the nun gave her a statue of the Sacred Heart of Jesus. Today, with her modern (non-denominational) Bible, she looked back at this episode with incredulity.

All this is sheer gain. What is not gain is the decline in religious practice, and the substitution for active participation of watching religious programmes on television. If the churches are to react to this decline, then they must continue to wrestle with their traditions, especially those from the formative period. The evidence above from New Testament theologians is that Jesus was concerned with preaching the Kingdom, as a way of demonstrating the nature of the God which now confronted Israel. The answer which Jesus gave to the diverse and confused world of the New Testament was one of a God who was present in daily life, alongside those who were unforgiven, unhealed and devalued. Yet this was not a message simply of good works and social care. Far more fundamentally, it expressed the initiative of God in the world which was made by Him. In Jesus, the love of God takes concrete shape in the world. Those who follow Him are called to cross boundaries and be active in the world, as a sign of God's valuing of ourselves. Through this activity God can be known.

All this may not fill the churches in Sunderland. I will come in the next two chapters to the question of personal evangelism. But towns like Sunderland no longer need reports and commissions on the way forward, however useful and productive at the time. The most a theological study of mission can do is suggest what the nature of Christian mission ought to be, in the light of the impact of mass secularization and of the New Testament. So three questions arise about the local church when we ask about boundaries and mission drawing together the evangelism of our secular society and the New Testament.

First, there is the organization of the local church. Is it a church run on rules: in order to belong, you must do this and that? There is no longer a strict divide between Catholic legalism and Protestant freedom. Many Protestant groups now have the practice of "disciplining". Members are given someone to watch over them, and they in turn watch over someone else. Jobs, marriages, hobbies and personal relationships are measured according to strict criteria, even if these laws are not written down and there to be consulted. The defence of this practice is that it provides "discipline, stability and reassurance in coping with life". The critics, however, see the practice as like George

Orwell's study of tyrannical brainwashing, *1984*: and they quote former leaders of the movement who describe the suffocating sense of inadequacy, despair and submission.

It is not the case that churches can exist without any rules. The fate of some early Christian groups shows both the weakness of this position, and the inevitability of conflict. Indeed, another strand of current New Testament research, which is not concerned with Jesus' preaching of the Kingdom, has instead looked at the power struggles in the church which followed Jesus. The issue must be what form the cohesion of the church will take as an institution and who holds the authority in the church. An alternative way of describing the local church is not in terms of rules, but in terms of relationships (belonging to St Mary's is about knowing Jesus in your life). Relationships again are simply not enough. But the balance between rules and relationships will be discovered as we attend to concerns with the drains of the church building, or a desire to exorcise demons. Churches interact with the world at the level of language they choose – drains or demons; flower rotas or friendship with AIDS sufferers. Sometimes we will speak of the local church as buildings, institutions and legal requirements, such as banns of marriage. Sometimes we will speak of the local church as people living with hopes and fears; sometimes as the invisible "church" across time and space, the communion of saints gathered around the power of the cross. Such language of saints, and time and space, again is not necessarily Roman Catholic. The influence of the German theologian D. Bonhoeffer lay not only in his commitment to a Christianity in the world but also in his contemporary expression of the communion of saints and the community life of monks and nuns.

The language of organization is drawn from modern science. Science breaks material down into the lowest levels possible, using the disciplines of biochemistry; atomic physics; molecular biology. But you can also speak of entities at a higher level, such as a human being as someone with psychological drives and feeling. Systems thinking has emerged to handle these different levels of describing the same object. It is, however, a crucial requirement for any church engaged in mission that it knows what level it is operating at. This is not a book on "how to engage in successful mission", but the growth of Mission Audits and other forms of stringent self-examination is crucial. It is at least arguable that some of the aspects of church life we examined in Sunderland were indeed the defence of a past culture, which is not to be patronized but not confused with the Gospel either.

The second question a local church should ask is in terms of its energy. Things are bound together by energy, which forms and shapes each entity. Animals interact with their world by processing light, heat and matter; they also use the energy of language. Human beings have social and political structures. Information is the exchange of energy within a system, which is formed and shaped energy – such as speech. But what energy has the Church? There is the dynamic growth from the old pre-Christian life to the new. The relationship of the local church to the universal Church is critical here, as well, and will be taken up in the final chapter on mission and unity. However, the dynamic, powerful, vibrant forces in the local church can be deeply destructive as well. The growth of psychological awareness in the churches has given rise to a number of books which explain the apparently pointless feuds which fester inside churches, or relate worship to the inner experiences of rejection, pain and hurt. It is at this point above all that honesty is needed. Is the energy destructive of constructive? Is it best described as the energy of forgiveness, empowered by the Spirit, or is it a form of social exclusion? At its best the creative energy should affirm the importance of the members of a church (black or white, rich or poor, male or female) in their personal histories, while transcending these categories as well by the universal love of God, revealed in the preaching and life of Jesus and still expressed today. At its worst, the vacuous language of pious religiousity smothers that which most needs to be affirmed.

"Who one is does not matter for one is a Christian." This false reconciliation is destructive of personal identity. But, as with the preaching of Jesus, mission as energy is not just affirmation of personal identity but a revealing (in and through this affirmation) of the energy of God: the making known the presence of the eternal in time.

The third question that should be asked of the local church, after the issues of language and organization on the one hand, and energy on the other, is that of openness to the world. What degree of openness has your local church to the world? A thermostat reacts to heat by opening up or closing the boiler. How do we control the interaction of church and world, in terms of feedback? Does the church listen to the world? Yet it is not the case that churches can simply have their agendas set by the world. Systems must have boundaries. A stone just lies there, plants are open to the environment. Some people believe you can talk to plants. I remember a lady in East London who prayed by her first-floor window-box. The plants grew beautifully, though I could never bring myself to make the connection. Human beings are open to the past, to people, to nature. But once you are open, you need to handle the information which will flow in. Otherwise the whole system breaks down.

Canon James Anderson, the Mission Secretary of the Church of England, has written:

> It has always proved impossible to define boundaries for the church e.g. the long and sterile debate about the visible as opposed to the invisible church. Attempts to define never seem to work. Probably this is because Church people are always also people in society; conversely, who do you exclude from the church or at least where do you draw the line between "people of goodwill" and Christian? Perhaps we need to think of boundaries as types of "exchangers" e.g. heat-exchangers or walls of a womb. In these cases boundaries are means of communication to enable heat to pass from one area to another

or food from one being to another – means of communication rather than barriers.

Conclusion

I do not think that it is profitable to define "mission" in the abstract. What is needed is an approach which covers three areas, in the familiar model of theological reflection. First, we need to begin with a concrete example. In my case it was a review of the Methodist Church in Sunderland. Secondly, we need to examine this by using criticial disciplines, such as sociology, and review why churches have declined. Is the secularization thesis helpful or not? Thirdly, this must be held against the resources of the Christian tradition, and in particular the teaching of Jesus, as recorded in Scripture. Finally, we need to get some goals for action. I have resisted doing the last of these. This is not a book on how to engage in mission, but on why it is of concern to the churches. However, there are three key questions for the local church at this stage.

First, there is the question of its organization and language: what a church believes about its worship, and the ideals which should govern its inner life will determine the nature of its mission more than anything else. Organization is not simple but complex, operating on many levels. Secondly, there is the understanding this church has of what empowers it. John Riches's study of Jesus' ministry always relates his activity to the underlying dynamic of the creative presence of God in the midst of suffering and conflict. Only this gave the necessary assurance which carried him into death. But power or energy within a church can be destructive or creative. Thirdly, there is the degree of openness to the world. Does the church just lie there in the community, hardly affecting it at all, as slugs crawl over an inert stone which is a barrier in their path? Or is there so much openness that the church dissolves into the world, as a chemical merges with the liquid into which it passes, losing its own identity?

Organization; energy; openness. If the churches are to survive into the twenty-first century, and that it is surely not a rhetorical statement in some areas but a deeply serious one, these must be the central issues. Mission, then, is that following of the ministry of Jesus which is not only true to life but true to His life: true to life in that it is aware of the need constantly to be in dialogue with the world and its needs; true to His life in that it acts for the glory of that God Whose love was revealed in Christ.

The implications for action will be traced throughout the remaining chapters. As the Church changes yet further in the next century, the increasing variety of responses to the surrounding community will place greater and greater stress on its identity and common life. One response would be to limit the openness to the world: that response, common enough in local churches, would be disastrous. Instead a deeper stress on understanding why the Church is the way it is, from the energy which empowers it (in conventional language, using the tradition as a living force), will allow more flexibility and experimentation in the mission of the Church. Some will work, while others will fail badly. The local church and the universal Church interact in many ways and on many levels: through all the changes which will occur in the future life of the Church in an increasingly secular society, it will not always be easy either to see a common Christian pattern. But the description of the Church as one, holy, Catholic and apostolic is a statement of faith. Because Christ is one and holy, we dare to speak of the Church as one and holy, despite its failings. Because Christ is universal and sent the Church, the Church can be called Catholic and apostolic. Finally, these are statements about the future Kingdom, when God's rule will be all in all. They are therefore statements of hope. It is in that hope that the Church is sent in mission to follow the way of Christ in an ever more secular world.

CHAPTER 3

Rejecting God

Barbed wire enclosed an arbitrary spot
  Where bored officials lounged (one cracked a joke)
And sentries sweated, for the day was hot:
  A crowd of ordinary decent folk
  Watched from without and neither moved nor spoke
As three pale figures were led forth and bound
To three posts driven upright in the ground.

The mass and majesty of this world, all
  That carries weight and always weighs the same
Lay in the hands of others; they were small
  And could not hope for help and no help came:
  What their foes liked to do was done, their shame
Was all the worst could wish; they lost their pride
And died as men before their bodies died.

> W. H. Auden, "The Shield of Achilles"

A God lonely, exiled, homeless in our sphere
Since his footfall breeds guilt, stirs dread,
Of a love fire-tongued, cleaving our sin
Retrieving the soul.

> Jack Clemo, "On the Death of Karl Barth"

Among the many studies of why people no longer "find God" in churchgoing and belonging to a church, two stand out in my mind. Both originated in the North-East, but the implications are much wider than that. One was a study of why working-class people in Sunderland find the Church irrelevant; the other was a study of ministry in Scotswood, Newcastle. Both are concerned with the old working class, which is very far from the new middle class who have flourished in the last decade. It is important to note this bias in the stories these studies tell.

Yet Leslie Francis and Michael Winter tell a similar story of the negative impact of religious education on young people. Knowing God through learning about him in school does not seem a way out either. Therefore this chapter must ask whether, in Robin Gill's phrase, there can be an answer beyond decline. I have argued in the last chapter that Britain is not a monochrome secular country but a deeply confusing pluralistic one with many forms of religious belief, private and public. The question to the churches is a dual one. It is not simply how one should try to resist the decline in church membership, and turn it round into church growth, but why one should do so. Therefore this chapter is incomplete until there is a consideration of why personal evangelism should be once again a priority for the churches. To put it at its bluntest, why does God matter in the modern world? It is significant that theologians like Stephen Sykes, Robert Jenson and George Lindbeck all address this issue in the recent collection of essays *Keeping the Faith*; that Nicholas Lash can discuss evangelism alongside social witness in a recent issue of *Church Action on Poverty*; that Archbishop John Habgood can place the credibility of the Gospel as the key issue for the 1990s in his latest book. Evangelism is back on the theological agenda in a way not seen for many decades. But it will be a debate which may give different answers to "why mission?": not the least important point is that a pluralistic society will be offered a pluralism of theologies. There clearly are some limits to what is theologically within the Christian tradition, but any attempt to impose a straight down-the-line answer to the confused agnosticism of modern Britain will only prove counter-productive.

Sunderland and Scotswood

Phil Brown, who was a student on the Aston Training Scheme, testing his vocation to be ordained in the Church of England, put the point with typical forcefulness. In the next few pages I will quote extensively from his study of his friends in Sunderland. Phil Brown began his report by asking "Why my working class father-in-law, and many people like him, does not go to church and is anti-church?" Phil believed that there were many barriers between how working-class people recognized and expressed their experiences of God and the way the Church wanted them to, or expressed its belief in God. Yet he also believed that people outside the Church could both know God and indeed feel a need to express that experience or those feelings. What was it in the Church that prevented them expressing that experience and turned that need elsewhere?

Simply to ask the question is of course to immerse oneself in a vast discussion about religion and the working classes since the Industrial Revolution. Yet while it is important to build on this work, there is also an immediacy about the question which cannot simply be turned into a discussion. Indeed, there is a further point which follows on straight away. If one is working-class inside the church, must there be an element of compromise there? Again there is the qualification of "what denomination?", "what area?" – but the issue is a real one, despite the necessary qualifications.

So Phil wrote "Self worth – if you don't think much of yourself, then God cannot think much of you. When you've got nowt, you are nowt. Surely that cannot be right?"[1] Sunderland is a town with fierce local histories and loyalties. There is a tradition of "hatching, matching and despatching" in the town, where local clergy are asked "to do the bairn" at baptisms. The same is true of weddings and funerals. But while these events are real enough, that is where the place of the Church stops for most people. The Church is another world in which they see themselves as having no part. This is especially so if you are unemployed. Unemployment has long been high in Sunderland. So the unemployed man who said "I've got nowt, I am nowt and what does the Church mean to me? – Nowt" puts a belief in a way unfair to many parishes who have responded to unemployment with many different schemes – yet it is probably true enough. Sunderland has a belief that life is a bit of a struggle, and knows that it is seen as second-class. Therefore there is a fierce local pride, looking after one's own and a defensive but very strong local humour. There is long-suffering philosophy which has lasted for generations. Self-worth was and is determined by how you survive, and cope with wealth and possessions (or the lack of them). In this regard the Church is seen as linked to those who are well educated, and so churchgoing is linked to dress, speech and education.

Once, in Victorian and Edwardian England, churches ran many social clubs in Sunderland. Today those on long-term unemployment benefit either simply try to make ends meet, or, if there is money, spend it on a night out, especially if they are young. Therefore, in Phil Brown's words, "vicars are judged by how little they interfere in people's lives", though most local clergy were seen as approachable, and there if needed, in times of trouble. Yet there is an underlying fatalism present here – "it didn't matter if there is a God or not, because we're stuck with whatever we've got anyway." God is seen as above the emotional and physical level that most people live on. Relationships are not as open as they might be also – life skills and values are no longer passed on from old to young, as once they were. There appears to be increasing drunkenness with more leisure and the fear of suspected child abuse. The old way of life is changing, though it changes more slowly in Sunderland than in many places. There is much in the new way of life to give thanks for, but the changes are not easy.

Phil Brown notes that

> from a position of power the church has talked at the working

class for generations. Now that power has gone, and the working class have a power base of their own, independent of the church, partly through the welfare state and better education, they don't have to listen anymore... People are tired of promises and "pie in the sky". They are tired of being told Jesus can change their lives, only to find themselves being moulded into the image of lukewarm respectability. We must allow people to worship God within their own frames of reference and experience. How we do that is another matter, but getting rid of some of those hymns might be a start.

Phil Brown describes two interviews which he had on his project:

Interview – Fred*

Fred is a 24-year-old bachelor. He works as a waiter in a large hotel just outside Sunderland. He is quite easy going, has many friends, and spends a lot of his free time hiking and camping, for which he usually seeks out sponsors to aid various charities. He is also a keen supporter of Greenpeace, lives at home with his parents and sister, and is a self confessed draught Guinness addict.

In our time together it was at times difficult to cut through Fred's flippant manner, but I discovered that this was not put on, but to some extent part of his way of coping with a lousy job with lousy pay, and questions about life he maintains are "beyond him".

Fred's family have no history of church involvement and he doesn't know who his local vicar is. He believes that the T.V. portrayal of Church of England vicars is rubbish but sees the church as irrelevant – "I never bother with it. I'd rather be out enjoying meself. You can't prove anything anyway." On a

*name changed from the real one

lighter note, Fred wondered what was the point of going to heaven anyway – "All the ones that make life fun are not going to be there" and he mentioned Samantha Fox and the Rolling Stones.

The main part of our discussion centred around two comments Fred made. Firstly he said that even if there is or isn't a God, it doesn't matter as we're still in the same situation. Secondly, he said "We're stuck here, and it's all up to us." I felt that both these comments related directly to the church which, if, as Christ's body here and now, is or is seen to be, irrelevant, then God becomes irrelevant. If Christians are seen to be less than dynamic in living their faith then the God they serve can't be much cop. "I'd rather go on a CND march than go to church at least you're trying to do something."

Fred feels the Church of England fits very well with Mrs Thatcher's way of thinking because "you don't see many poor people in church, and they all go by car."

Fred claims to "hate" some people but feels he does try to help others when he can.

Two weeks after this interview I met with Fred again, to try to feed back to him, through my Christian experience and reflection, what he had said to me. Because I know him quite well, I was able to take certain chances in what I said, knowing that, rather than take offence, he would just tell me I was talking rubbish.

I began by suggesting Fred has had some experiences of God, which as I expected, he denied. I asked him how he felt and what he thought about when he was out hiking over the moors, and why he was bothered about raising money for other people, and together we began to strip away some of the hard and fast rules that we obey when we attempt to translate a natural experience of, and yearning after, God.

I hope Fred got as much out of our meetings as I did. What began as one interview developed into a sharing and a seeking after God, away from the jargon and process of the church. I have come to see that I was involved (and still am) in evangelism in my relationship with Fred, but in a way I had rarely experienced before, that is, meeting him where he is, and drawing out God from those things he can relate to, rather than charging in Bible in hand, and bashing his ears with doctrine and spiritual blackmail.

Interview – Mavis

Mavis is in her mid 20s. She works in an office and lives at home with her parents.

Mavis says she does not believe in God, although she is Church of England. The last time she went to church was two years ago for a relative's wedding. "It was alright I suppose."

She is not sure that the church has any class distinction within it but says, "I'm not convinced by any aspect of the church at all."

Mavis hopes to be married sometime next year, and this will take place in her local church as, "it will be a day to remember and the registry office doesn't give the wedding that a church does." Her wedding will have nothing to do with God, although she won't tell the vicar that. She thinks he would still marry them, as he needs the money. Her local vicar is "canny" and she thinks she could go to talk to him if she wanted to, but never would, as she sees her family as being the place where things are sorted out. When problems arise, her family close ranks.

"Jesus was a person but it all got exaggerated. The Bible was written down so long afterwards it can't be factual. I suppose he wanted just to help people but the legend grew. A thousand years from now it could be Tony Benn." (Mavis is a staunch socialist.)

"There's nothing after death. You've got to make the best of what you've got."

Mavis spends her money on clothes and "a good night out at the boat" (the Tuxedo Princess, a floating disco on the River Tyne in Newcastle).

A similar story of the rejection of "finding God" in the Church is told in Hazel Ditchburn's study of Scotswood. Scotswood, in Newcastle, is a community very hard hit by depression. Hazel Ditchburn worked there for several years in the 1980s as an Anglican deaconess (later deacon).[2] She speaks of the relationship of church and community as both feeling "trapped in a cycle of deprivation ... which mirror each other." Scotswood bears the stress of much of the surrounding area, in high levels of unemployment and pathological depression. In practice this means "financial problems, vandalism and crime, mental illness and peer pressure". There is a clear link between social deprivation and ill health: "it is common after a parochial visit for children to hang onto or run alongside my car, and unfortunately road accidents are very high among the group." Play is dangerous and often badly supervised; gardens resemble rubbish tips strewn with glass and cans. Overall the area has an unemployment rate of 38% (1985); in some streets it is 80%. There is heavy dependence on tranquillizer drugs, and many people have long histories of emotional disorder. There is a subculture of acceptable crime; much indebtedness; and broken marriages. Two instances are mentioned by Hazel Ditchburn. She writes about the funeral of a baby, and the single parent.

> Death brings out more basic dilemmas too; very often deep-seated but that may also say something about the spiritual/psychological make up of those involved. I refer to those situations when "cot death" or similar occurs and the parents remain convinced there has been some "Evil" or "Psychic" presence in the home at the time. Strong smells, apparitions, mists and premonitions have all been mentioned to me at such times. It can be particularly difficult to untangle the many

different factors involved i.e. superstition, hearsay, dabbling with the occult, psychological "hang ups" before or during the process of arranging a funeral. Where this occurs with a young unmarried couple the whole gambit or relationships is involved, and it can be particularly difficult for the young people to continue with their relationship after the funeral and often they drift apart.

Mary and Wayne were just such a couple. They lived together since Mary had become pregnant and I first met them when I was asked to take the funeral of baby Wayne aged nine months. Wayne was uncommunicative with me and it was left to Mary to explain their fears surrounding the death. Apparently about six weeks before they had begun to feel uneasy in their council house, smelling strange damp smells and particularly around the babies cot. They complained to the council and asked for an exchange. The next situation was that they felt they could see a light flitting back and forward over the cot. They experimented with curtains etc. but the light remained. These situations continued until the morning Mary found Wayne dead in his cot. The death itself brought to a head Mary's guilt at living with Wayne and not being married and also the fact that she had never told her father of the baby's existence (her mother was dead and she had an older sister). Wayne became more and more withdrawn as I visited them after the funeral and eventually they both were living in a makeshift way at Wayne's sister's around the corner, sleeping in armchairs and just going around to their own house each morning to check it. Mary asked me to go and say some prayers with her in the house as she wanted to go back, which I did, but in the end Wayne wouldn't return and they put in for an exchange with the council to an estate in the north of Newcastle which they eventually got.

While the psychic phenomenon is an aberrational thing in any society it can be found particularly in the West End of Newcastle (as perhaps it can be found in pockets in many cities). Many people in the West End who are groping for "kicks" have been to "spuggies" (Spiritualists) seances etc. The residue of tribal Christian belief, tradition and superstition that is found in working class culture and often labelled folk religion takes on a new perspective in urban areas where religion also encompasses psychic forces.

Yet the richness and variety of relationships excites and bewilders me. Grandparents, children and grandchildren and the whole network of aunties and cousins can be seen to "pull together" to make sense of life, particularly when perhaps they have in a combined effort nursed one of their number through a terminal illness determined that it is "family" work. The feelings of strength, joy and shared loss – characteristics by no means purely "Geordie" – that are involved can be felt along with their determination, pride and tenacity.

Birth (along with death) is the great family event with the gathering together of the extended family making their way to church for baptism, a sacrament still widely used in Scotswood. It seems in this fast changing world to give some sense of order and normality in the lives of those who are sustaining change and chaos in terms of their employment, relationships and livelihood. It is at baptism that I can observe the "celebration" of life that is so essential for human beings. At baptism all the "stops" are pulled out, best clothes, baby "rigged out" in gown and veil, men fresh from their Sunday drinking in the club (still primarily a male preserve on Sunday morning) are chivvied to church to see the "bairn done". The other side of this coin is the single parent – usually very young girl who, desperate for adulthood and recognition which she cannot find in unemployment or peer groups becomes pregnant to prove herself, not thinking of the years ahead of the responsibility of parenthood, of the financial complications, but taking affirmation where she can find it, usually with a young lad in the same position as herself, resulting in her being left "holding the baby" yet still wanting to celebrate usually with baptism, her new status as a mother. Ahead lies the loneliness of living in a council flat provided with financial help from the "social", sleepless nights and directionless days – all this at 17 years of age tries the resilience of the strongest character and yet they survive.

There are also feelings of strength and loyalty, dedicated teachers, and community policing. There are many facilities for those unemployed, but what is striking is the way a vigorous family life and attempts to cope with the pressure of poverty and unemployment are threatened by repeated depression, and personal breakdown.

Women, often with a string of children already, continually find themselves pregnant and seeking abortion or sterilization after many pregnancies when in fact with adequate family planning these situations need not have occurred. Women continue to be drudges at a young age allowing use of their bodies as "baby machines" regardless of the great toll this takes on their physical and psychological well being. This very often breeds a resentment to the children they do have leading to neglect, child abuse and misery.

Death, especially cot death, leads to a belief in the occult, superstition and psychic phenomena. These stresses and strains are accentuated by the "advertising of consumer goods, soap operas and glossy images [which] present them with an alternative lifestyle which is unattainable".

The issue for the church is not simply relieving unemployment or reducing poverty. It is encouraging people to take strength for their own future, aided by those who are inspired by a Christian vision which they may share with those around them in a way which is never patronizing. Equally the task of the church's mission is to combat superstition, depression and the burden of psychic phenomena – since this false spiritualism drags down further those who are already the ones least able to bear the stresses of poverty and ill health.

But in fact the attitude of the congregation is seen as defensive about the vast Victorian church building. The congregation is small and overworked. Members commented on the past ministry of the clergy in terms which are amusing, but also revealed how central the clergy had been in past decades. It was a constant feature of their comments that the congregation did what the vicar asked of them. Equally the congregation increasingly had unfulfilled expectations of their clergy, perhaps becoming dependent on them.

> Vicars kept changing so that they didn't manage to keep up to date with the comings and goings of the people, and a lot depended on the vicar's attitude.

> The change in worship with Series 2 and 3 lost a lot of people – a lot of things have happened to make people fed up. There was a health epidemic and a few children died including some of the church children – in some cases the Vicar didn't seem to care. Even the money changed to decimals and the giving went down again.

> Vicars have been a problem. Some hindered the ministry in Scotswood; some stuck to the Bible too much; some talked above your head and some weren't in touch with ordinary folk.

There is an enormous struggle to keep the church building in reasonable repair. The fence was frequently vandalized, and there was great concern about keeping the children out of the church grounds. Equally there were long discussions on whether to sell the church hall. The congregation varied from twenty to thirty most weeks, with fifty at Christmas and Easter. Evensong is now a past memory, for the congregation ages. Income remains a problem.

What is most difficult to achieve is a sense that the church is reaching out to the community. Individual members are strongly involved through centres for the young unemployed, playgroups, etc. Is this not enough then? In one way it certainly is. But it is also the case that the church as a local community should be more than the individual work of its members, inspiring though that is. What is needed is some policy of outreach, in terms of either communal involvement and social action, or visiting. Yet the pressure on the congregation is that of memories of the past, anxiety about the future and a preservation of the buildings inherited from an earlier generation. Appeals for a deeper commitment can produce the following comment: "I've stopped going to church on some Sundays because I've just got a pound left till family allowance on Tuesday that has to buy a loaf of bread and a bottle of milk, and I feel guilty if I don't go and put anything in the collection."

Youth

We move now to setting these stories in a wider context of national surveys of young people. Dr Leslie Francis is an Anglican priest and psychologist, who has worked on children's attitude to religion since the early 1970s. Leslie Francis's work measured the degree of favourableness towards religion which a pupil at school had developed.[3] This is not the same as an appreciation of the religious (or "deeper") dimension of life. It is possible to understand (in the broadest sense of the term) what is meant by religious experience, and to know emotionally the implications of religious faith. Yet a person could feel negatively towards that experience, and respond to his or her understanding in ways not simply critical but also deeply unfavourable. It is of course possible to give an account of life where understanding the depths of human experience is seen as "faith" and must be a source for wonder, always drawing out a positive response. For a humanist who rejects religion may have an appreciation of life which has integrity and deep courage. There are humanists who construct "cases of significance which offer him a temporary home in the desert which surrounds him." But "there is no 'answer' to evil and death. They are the other side of good and life. They are ultimate facts and they must be accepted as such." But such humanists, while the allies of Christians working in areas of deprivation, still reject God. Does this matter? Or are they simply to be seen as having a different world view without God?

Leslie Francis's work concentrated on how children felt about "six specific aspects of the Christian religion, which would be meaningful even to a young child. These are God, Jesus Christ, the Church, prayer, the Bible and Christian teaching or worship in schools." Leslie Francis was not then concerned with humanism, or moral development, but with attitudes to Christianity in children. Whether children had a depth or quality of life was not the point. Putting it in this stark manner may make the issue of belief far too simple, but it does make the point with great clarity. Do they believe in a good God?

When Dr Francis studied children from the first year of the junior school to the fifth year of the secondary school, he found that there was a "steady and persistent decline in attitude towards Christianity". This was in denominational state schools, and the deterioration was consistent throughout a child's growing up. It did not increase with adolescence, with the move to secondary school, or with new ways of thinking. Quite simply, the older children got, the less they were favourable to Christianity. A simple statement such as "I know that God helps me" provides an example. Of the first-year juniors 79 per cent felt positively towards this statement. In the next three years the figures were 72, 71 and 54 per cent. In the first year of the secondary school the figure was 46 per cent. By the fifth year, only 27 per cent of pupils felt that God helped them. The majority denied any experience of God's help in life. The decline in religious belief was therefore consistent over time, although it was a slow process.

The 1974 study quoted here also noted that the decline greatly accelerated after the age of fifteen. Between fifteen and sixteen, during the final year of compulsory schooling when the attitudes which persist into adult life are often created, children's attitudes deteriorated most. There is a reason for this, but it is again negative. If children were involved in a church, or felt that they were involved, then they were far more likely to feel positive. The problem, of course, is that the decline in churchgoing among children is as acute as the deterioration in attitudes. It is difficult to answer the question of whether children cease to attend because their attitudes are changing, and thus church (or the various Sunday schools, children's activities, etc.) is seen as boring; or whether non-attendance produces more estranged attitudes, in which they simply do not feel any gut sympathy with religious activity or belief at all. Either way, Dr Francis's survey shows that church attendance and sympathy to religion decline in roughly equal degree from eight to sixteen years old.

This 1974 survey shows with considerable force that most school-leavers from state schools enter the adult world with an attitude towards the existence of God which is deeply antagonistic to traditional Christian teaching. At the very least, Jesus taught people to trust in "the fatherhood of God and the brotherhood of man", in Harnack's phrase from *The Essence of Christianity*. "Consider the ravens: they neither sow nor reap, they have neither storehouse nor barn, and yet God feeds them. Of how much more value are you than the birds" (Luke 12:25). It is this belief which children reject overwhelmingly by the age of sixteen, whatever their commitment to social justice and personal integrity.

The 1974 survey was repeated in 1978. The trends were the same, but were observed in children a year younger than in the previous survey. Thus, among fourth-year secondary pupils in 1974 47 per cent believed God listened to their prayers; in 1978, that figure was 38. In 1974 62 per cent of that age-group believed God helped them; in 1978 52. Church services were found boring by 42 per cent in 1974; by 49 in 1978. And the Bible was seen as out of date by 13 per cent in 1974; by 22 in 1978.

Figures can be wearying. It is sufficient to say that the study was repeated a third time in 1982, and the figures had deteriorated further. Furthermore, the 1978 survey also looked at attitudes towards school and games, history, maths, music and English lessons. None of these reflected the same disenchantment, except for music. Thus it is not the case that pupils become disenchanted with school and that religious disenchantment reflects this. Children may put school behind them at sixteen or eighteen, but it is not in itself boring, irrelevant or untrue. Some aspects of school life may be like this, and some pupils might reject school, but on the whole the 1960s vision of a need to de-school society is not held by young people. It is quite clear, however, that religious assemblies and compulsory religious education as part of the regular curriculum do not appeal to young people, except in a minority probably linked in one way or another to a church. When the questions about "which religion?" and "which faith?" are added to this disenchantment, it is probable that the 1988 Education Act will not produce greater commitment to the churches or to Christianity on the part of young people. Not only is it doubtful if greater resources in terms of specialist religious studies teachers could turn the tide, there is an entire set of questions on what is appropriate in a pluralist, multi-faith culture.

Leslie Francis sums up the implication of his work as follows.

Once the churches accept the notion that they are living in a post-Christian society in which education has become secularized, they need also to accept the responsibility for developing a theology of education within an alien culture. Such a theology of education needs to be neither defeatist nor totally separatist. The strength and distinctiveness of the Christian gospel often emerges most powerfully when the tension between gospel and society is properly identified.[4]

The comment about an alien host culture reflects deep-seated disagreements between Dr Francis and secular philosophers of education, whose work has been very influential in state schools. But whatever the merits of that particular argument, there can be little doubt that pupils are not made Christian by daily state school education. They enter adult life deeply agnostic about the reality of God as anything more than a vague presence in their lives.

One final piece of evidence (on young people) is found within the Roman Catholic community. There have been historians such as Alan Gilbert who have argued that the Roman Catholic community provides the only real religious group with a belief in God which is not influenced by deistic, or entirely liberal, presuppositions. Again the evaluation which Gilbert provides of liberal theology is one which I would want to dispute strongly. But the crucial refutation of Gilbert's argument is provided by Michael Winter's study of young Roman Catholics in his book *Whatever Happened to Vatican Two?* In the chapter "Handing it on to the next generation", he examines similar sociological studies of Roman Catholic schools to Dr Francis's study of state schools. (There is, incidentally, a great deal more research by Dr Francis on church schools, both Anglican and Roman Catholic. I have quoted the three surveys of state schools because they are the most striking, and for reasons of brevity.)

Michael Winter gives a summary of the evidence which he gathers in this chapter.

> Many young people aged about twenty, who were brought up in Catholic families, hold views on religion and morals, which are so much at variance with the implied presuppositions of Bishops' Pastoral Letters, for example that we must acknowledge the existence of a credibility gap of staggering propor-

tions. The lack of adequate sociological investigation in this field is distressing since it shows a lack of pastoral concern, but the phenomenon is so widespread and so unmistakable that we are justified in studying it despite the paucity of scientific evidence. The parochial clergy, and enlightened lay people have all recognized instances of widespread abandonment of Christianity. The kind of thing which I have in mind is the situation of Catholic families, where both parents are committed members of the church, but whose children have all, or nearly all, abandoned the practice of religion. The most obvious sign of their attitudes is the complete abandonment of mass and the sacraments; they may also deliberately refuse to marry the person with whom they are living, even after the birth of children. But what is significant is that these rejections of institutional religion may well be accompanied by a high sense of moral responsibility in other areas, total fidelity to their parents, and sincere concern for all that concerns the well-being of persons.[5]

Winter quotes a number of surveys, the most recent of which is from summer 1982. In Plymouth 165 young people whose mothers were members of the Catholic Women's League returned questionnaires. It was a restricted sample, but one of great interest, for the CWL is an organization of deeply committed Catholics. Furthermore Plymouth is an area where Catholics are in a minority, and so without the extensive Catholic school system found in London. Of the 165 aged from sixteen to thirty, only 59 per cent went to mass on a regular basis. Much higher percentages disagreed with the Vatican on divorce, pre-marital sex and contraception. As with Dr Francis's research, the question arises as to whether the influence of a Catholic school is cause or effect of religious conviction, and more especially the lack of conviction in the 41 per cent who had lost regular touch with the Church as an institution. The researchers from the University of London commented:

> Careful study was made of the type of schooling to see whether young people attending Catholic primary and Secondary Schools were more likely to continue practising their faith, than those sent to non-Catholic schools. The survey found no evidence to this effect: there was no appreciable difference between the two as far as continuity of practice was concerned.

Catholic schooling then was ineffectual. What was not helpful at all was the attitude of the parish priest, and young people's disillusionment about a religion which practices "isolation from everyday life" in the rules which govern priestly existence. Thus religion was seen as irrelevant.[6]

Nor does private education provide a different answer. Although the survey was criticized for its sampling, the Catholic Chaplain at the University of Cambridge noted how few products of the Catholic public schools actually attended mass in a November 1983 survey. The figures are probably too arbitrary to be worth repeating, but Michael Winter, who spent seven years as Catholic Chaplain to the University of London, echoes the sceptical comment of the Cambridge chaplain.

> The figures make nonsense of the claim of Catholic public schools that they are forming Christian gentlemen who will be the future leader of lay Catholic opinion and action . . . very good company, immensely likeable, and totally impervious to the Gospel.

Finally, it is worth mentioning a 1973 survey by the eminent Catholic sociologist Dr Hornby-Smith. He surveyed the fifth form of three Catholic comprehensive schools in the south of England, with 419 responses. One London LEA comprehensive provided a basis of comparison. The pupils had to range themselves on a six-point scale from complete belief in God, without doubts, to no belief in God. The first three points could broadly be described as believing, although the third expressed belief only at some times in life in the existence of God. The three Catholic schools scored 78, 78 and 76 per cent as "believers": the LEA school recorded 47 per cent. (Dr Francis's figures in 1974 recorded 27 per cent of the same age-range who believed in a God who helped them.) But there was much greater dissent on the divinity of Jesus among young Catholics. Even when those with "some doubts" were included, the three Catholic schools only recorded 59, 51 and 41 per cent. The LEA school showed 25 per cent. Clearly as a basis for religious practice and attendance at mass, these figures show massive disenchantment. There would be many who "with doubts" would accept that "basically Jesus is Divine" but feel alienated from institutional religion, and never attend mass at all. Fifteen years later the figures would almost certainly be lower. Finally, it must be remembered that the teenagers of this 1974 survey would now be married and have families. If the emphasis for the child's religious upbringing rests on parental commitment, then parents who have no belief in Jesus as divine are not likely to teach their children differently. Even if it is argued that people with young families sometimes come back to more religious belief after the rebellions of adolescent life, a feeling that "Jesus was a great man" but not "the Son of God any more than all of us are" is a limited premise to base that hope on. Dr Hornby-Smith noted the great antagonism among young Catholics to "official", institutional religion, with an impoverished idea of God which led to the rejection of belief as "childish" in adolescence. Above all he recorded the sheer lack of support from family or peer groups, which led to a "drift" from religion. There was seldom a conscious choice or decision, but instead a struggle for personal autonomy by young people which led to the slow abandonment of religion for a deeply institutional privatized religion. This of course leads into a cycle of religious decline where each generation brings up children with less belief in traditional Christian claims about God, who themselves hand on less and less to the next generation.[7]

Suburbia

We have looked at young people in Sunderland, at national surveys of young people by Leslie Francis and at surveys of young Roman Catholics nationally. The difficulty of being an inner-city church in Newcastle has also been described. What has not been mentioned until now is the suburban church. It is in suburbia that many evangelical churches are growing, and in general the position of all the churches is much easier here. But even in this area the account of two Anglican churches' activity in Hartlepool and Chilton is striking. The vicar in Hartlepool said in a conference on mission in the 1980s:

> AN ATTEMPT TO FORM AN "OUTPOST". Part of our Parish is an up-market private development, where mortgages are the absorbing interest, no one is evident during the day, and where membership is of the Cricket Club, Rotary, Soroptomists, etc rather than of the Church. Marriages and Baptisms are few because the age-range of the residents is wrong for occasional offices. We have tried several times to build on the few staunch Christians in the neighbourhood by using a "coffee-evening" ploy, by inviting people to attend house-groups, by getting "our" people to call on and talk to their non church-going friends and neighbours. Zero. People are polite but dismissive. They have made it clear to the Head Teacher of the local Primary School that no religious teaching of the sort that might result in commitment will be acceptable, and to our initiatives there has been a firm negative. We thought of setting up church at the school (no dice – head teacher) or at the Cricket Club: but since all the people who might be part of such a congregation have at least one car, and could travel to church with no trouble anyway, talk at the door or on the living-room settee is not welcome. So this is an area of failure – suggestions would be gratefully received!

A similar story was told in Chilton, a small village in the centre of Durham.

> The parish of Chilton has mixed housing, both council and private. The council housing is situated in the well-established areas of the parish, whilst the private housing tends to be on the fringe of the parish. The latest building work saw a new Wimpey Homes Housing Estate come into being.
> At a PCC meeting the members discussed what could be done to make people of the parish more aware of what the church was all about and what it had to offer. The meeting decided that it would split the parish up into sectors, and each sector would be dealt with in turn. The sector first to be touched was to be that comprising the new Wimpey housing estate, since no sustained contact had been made with the people of that estate other than spasmodic visiting by myself (no contact at all under my predecessor).
> They then went on to discuss how to do this. The meeting decided that a letter of invitation should be sent to every house on that estate, in which the residents were invited to come and have coffee with members of the PCC. At that meeting various people would then present to those present what the Church had to offer both spiritually and socially. A copy of the parish magazine was also sent out with the letter.
> All this was done and the meeting was held. The response from the residents was abysmal. Three young mothers turned up. But the meeting went ahead as planned. The three who turned up were themselves surprised at the low response, for they thought it was a wonderful idea and a way of showing that the church cared and wanted to know you. Since that meeting those three young mums have become more committed and active in the worship and work of the church. As for those taking part the whole evening was very salutary, making many of them think for the first time what the church was all about.

In conclusion I would say this. Despite the lack of numbers from this our first attempt, it was felt that we should not be disheartened or give up, for lessons had been learned, both in preparation and presentation, and that next time we should take on a more well-established sector of the parish.

The two attempts do not show that all attempts at evangelism are doomed to failure, nor did either of the parish clergy argue this. These were initial attempts, in areas into which people had recently moved. Other strategies, such as contact through children, may have different results. What they both reflect, however, is the privatization of religion. In one of his earlier books, *Church and Nation in a Secular Age*, Archbishop John Habgood discusses how our society is increasingly privatized. It is not just a religious phenomenon, for anonymity and impersonality are features of everyday existence, as in shopping in a supermarket. Religion, however, takes the phenomenon much further. Belief is a matter of private choice, not a social function. The assumptions of the society where one lives are indifferent to religious faith. To some extent, of course, religion has always involved personal choice: the Jewish and Christian Scriptures show this clearly enough. What is different in Western Europe, and especially Protestant Western Europe, in the last decades of this century is the extent to which society offers no public framework to judge religion. What you choose is up to you. A second difference is the range of choice, with a vast variety of faiths to offer.

As John Habgood says, privatized religion offers freedom of choice, encouraging personal autonomy, individuality, tolerance and creative change. The difficulty is that it encourages an indifference to social questions, and an erosion of general criteria of truth. If all religious choice is arbitrary, why choose at all? Parishes with large numbers of their population who are mobile will find folk religion does not cut much ice either. Customary practice flourishes where generations live alongside each other, and settled communities enshrine views about religion. Mobility encourages yet greater privatization. Thus those who were very active in a previous church may on moving give up going altogether. And churches which attempt to move people from a privatized lifestyle, with their own personal values and choices, into a communal existence, with a tradition of worship and belief which extends back far beyond the memory of any individual church member, will find that attempt very difficult. It is not religion as such which is being rejected, though it may be that as well. It is what is seen as the offer of very clear-cut beliefs and values from a community which often values the past more than the present, and corporate life (the church members) more than the individual. The rejection is not of God, or faith, or commitment (though a few claim to be convinced atheists – 10 per cent in Houpeten's survey of Holland mentioned later in this chapter). It is rather a choice for personal self-awareness, and aspirations, against the Church, which is not seen as assisting these goals.[8]

Summary: Great Britain

It is time to summarize the argument so far in this chapter. The previous chapter argued that Britain was not a country which did not believe in God, or even a secular society. The evidence is too complex for that, as David Martin's work shows. What matters is that churches are able to involve themselves in their society, as the ministry of Jesus of Nazareth indicated very clearly. The New Testament provides evidence of a ministry which changed people's understanding of God and brought into existence a community who believed in the mercy and love of God as the predominant features of their faith. Yet what this chapter shows is that while Britain may be neither a secular nor an anti-Christian culture, it is one in which a growing number of people find institutional religion quite irrelevant. There is goodwill to the churches in Sunderland, but very little belief that religion makes any difference to the ordinary business of life. This is especially striking among young people, as Phil Brown's study shows. It is impressionistic, but it is based on a lifetime of being brought up in the area. Nationally, the research of Francis and Hornby-Smith demonstrate this disenchantment with religion nationally among young people. Again more anecdotally, the evidence of Catholic university chaplains at London and Cambridge reveals equally striking lack of commitment among Catholic undergraduates, even when they have been to private Catholic schools with regular daily worship.

This evidence suggests that young people who attend in their thousands such festivals as Spring Harvest and Green Belt or go to Taizé are quite uncharacteristic of their generation. It is not merely that there is a vast disenchantment with the Church and with the practice of "official religion", but also that traditional theological beliefs in the activity of God for good, or the divinity of Jesus, also become much less clearly held. Thus, alongside the evidence of the last chapter that Britain is an increasingly pluralistic and complex religious culture, even without the entry of other religious faiths into Britain, there is also much greater uncertainty about what people actually believe, or what everyone else believes.

Pluralism; privatization; uncertainty; complexity – the task of the Church in the "decade of evangelism" in the 1990s is enormous. It is also the case that in some deprived inner-city areas, or in deeply rural ones, the Church will become entirely identified with the surrounding folk-culture. That appears to be the implication of the study of Scotswood and the Church there. The pressure on individuals is so great that the only task which matters is preserving the church building and ensuring the survival of the congregation. However it is precisely this which is likely most to alienate the surrounding population. For a while folk religion, and memories of charitable help in the past, especially during the 1930s Depression in the North-East, will keep the church congregation alive among older people, and ensure a fairly high number of weddings, infant baptisms and funerals. (One study contrasts the percentage of Anglican baptisms which are baptisms of infants in Carlisle (60 per cent) with those in London (15 per cent). But as the congregation becomes even older, and the asset to even the most minimal Christian beliefs in the rest of the population diminishes, folk religion must be a precarious support for such churches. In short, more congregations will close in inner-city and deeply rural areas, or be reduced to a small if deeply committed handful of people. Already there are clear signs of this happening to the Methodist presence in some inner-city and rural areas in North-East England; Methodism in North Northumberland or the Durham dales is a shadow of itself before 1914.

The European Dimension

The theologian Anton Houpeten records the same pattern across Western Europe. He notes the decline in regular church attendance in young West German Catholics from 50 per cent (1952) to 16 (1980). The number who hardly ever went to church increased in the same period from 27 to 60 per cent. Yet these were the children of Catholic families. Of those who rarely, if ever, went 60 per cent found worship quite irrelevant to their daily lives. The correspondence with the Francis and Hornby-Smith figures in England is striking. Houpeten argues that the German Catholic community is being assimilated in its youngest generation into the beliefs and values of the rest of non-religious Germany. A small minority will continue to practice their faith, but they will be increasingly a minority group of Catholics. Similar figures can be found in the Reformed Dutch churches, where belief in a personal God is held by only one third of church members. The same agnosticism is held about beliefs in Jesus' divinity and life after death; yet these are the beliefs of church members.[9]

Once again Houpeten denies that this means that people have any less idealism. However, the decline in churchgoing is common across Germany and Holland, and in a Dutch survey 91 per cent argued that Christian belief without going to church is quite possible: 81 per cent said that they belonged to a faith, 70 per cent still had their children baptized, and 51 per cent called themselves believers. But only 39 per cent of those over 35, and 23 per cent of those under 35, believed in the existence of a personal God at all. Only 23 per cent of Dutch Catholics went to church in 1981, and 13 per cent of Dutch Reformed church members in 1979.

Lack of belief in a personal God; lack of commitment to the Church or churchgoing; yet commitment to personal ideals and goodwill to the Christian faith, however defined – Houpeten's evidence fits English culture as much as Dutch or German. Houpeten writes that there is

> a gradual shift from church membership and, at a much more leisurely tempo, a departure from belief in God, and religion. This process can only be described as a gradual process of alienation from the church which in a second or third generation results in an almost complete absence of Christian inspiration and tradition. In one group only the personal significance of faith will decline, without much change in the way in which it is conceived; in another group, it is primarily the actual beliefs which come under pressure, although personally people still attach a good deal of importance to faith. The remarkable thing here is that there is not much difference between the way those who belong to the church and those who do not belong to the church look at life, i.e. in the complex of convictions and attitudes by means of which people give significance to their existence.[10]

In conclusion, it is clear that the rejection of the churches by many people who are young working-class, or live in conditions of great poverty, is very great. Elsewhere the churches are not rejected, but faith becomes more and more a private matter. The pattern is the same in Holland, West Germany and England. These are countries which share a common heritage of the Reformation and the development of a strong middle-class culture in the last two centuries. There have been many attempts to meet the challenge of a privatized, pluralist and secular society. Yet religious faith expressed by joining a Christian church has become in these countries dramatically the choice of a small minority.

Houpeten lists six reasons which are often given as to why the rejection of the Church has taken place. First, he lists a loss of the sense of transcendence, the holy, grace and a true relationship with God in prayer. Central to religious decline is decline in the longing for a personal God who can fulfil life – the issue which united Luther and Ignatius Loyola on either side of the Reformation four centuries ago. Secondly, there is the replacement of the true ideals of the Jesus movement with middle-class values, respectability and adherence to political power. Jesus in this view was critical of Pharisees and Zealots, Romans and those who fled the world. He founded a movement whose followers would not fight in the army or take people to court; and which preached love for all, including their enemies. Such a persecuted Church of the first few centuries needs to be reborn by the Church rejecting social privilege and too easy an accommodation with cultural norms. The only place left for the Church is to become a voluntary movement, with an option for the poor, gathered in small basic communities. A third interpretation points not to the Fatherhood of God as transcendent and the ultimate desire of life, nor to Jesus and His message of liberation, but to the Spirit. The Church has declined because it has become complicated, intellectual, cumbersome and remote – where feeling, bodily contact and togetherness are celebrated, the Church will grow. It is enthusiasm, healing, wholeness which people look for. They are found in parts of the Third World, in Pentecostal churches, in some Evangelical groups. Such an interpretation looks to the inspiration of the Spirit in worship in small groups, in relationships. The stress here is on freedom, experience, awareness of needs: the Gospel story is about the experience of salvation by the lame, blind and crippled. It is their experience as broken people of salvation now that is crucial. Two other explanations of decline are less theological than sociological. One looks to the methods of the Church. Reorganization, training, communication skills all seek to build up the Church. Unless the Church is more professional, little will be done. In an increasingly professional world, there is no place for amateurs. One aspect of this analysis looks to greater centralizaton and a more distinctive message. This is certainly the analysis offered by the Vatican in the 1980s, with a reinforced authority of church leaders, clearer church discipline and an end of confusion. In a privatized complex world the Church must take a public, clear-cut stand. The alternative viewpoint rejects the stress above on firm leadership as authoritarian. Better education and training lead to a stress on greater participation by its membership in worship, and in ministry in general. Conversations about the faith, the creation of groups, more dialogue instead of prejudice about other religions and the growth of involvement in all aspects of our society by church members which leads into a gradual conversion of self – all this is the antidote to decline.[11]

There is a final analysis which rejects all of these, yet is favourable towards religion. A church which wishes to be a world Church, and a Church for the world, must accept that it will become a victim of the process. If people in the West do have high ideals and yet reject the Church, which is a consistent feature of the surveys mentioned above, then the values of love, peace and justice are at least partly the result of the influence of the Church over the centuries. Houpeten quotes Gregory of Nyssa in developing this viewpoint. "Only God can begin from God. We can only begin from humanity, and in seeking one another presume and hope that God is seeking us. We need not begin from God. He does that himself. We must seek his creation." Therefore some Christians have argued that concern about church membership is the wrong place to start for mission. Instead we must begin with where we are placed. Perhaps the loss of membership is only apparent, perhaps not. What matters is to build up communities which continue to help others and serve the ideals of love, peace and justice. It is no surprise, then, that a recent study of Anglican Evangelicals showed that even in this constituency the concern for the Third World was causing the old-established missionary societies to be less central in the concerns of parishes. The study notes,

> It is quite clear that those who have grown up in the 1970s and 1980s have been much more evidently moved by the visual evidence of human physical need than they have by the traditional Evangelical gospel of "rescuing lost souls in darkness". If anything the balance may have swung too far in the direction of alleviating physical and material deprivation at the expense of the good news of redemption.[12]

Others would certainly ask if the only guests in the Kingdom of God are those who know that they are saved, and not those living in the highways and byways with needs which they have long since given up expecting people to care for. Houpeten's careful analysis of the varieties of Christian interpretation for the causes of decline and the way forward will be taken up in the succeeding chapters. There is no easy answer in opting for one or other of these solutions. As Peter Baelz has written,

> Christian prayer as well as Christian life is involved in and conditioned by the actualities of the world as it is. There is no magical transformation which ignores the conditions of history and of nature as they have come to be. There is in prayer itself the same tension between the "already" and the "not yet" as we have seen in the rest of Christian experience

> ... Although this faith comes to him as a gift – that is, he himself is unable to control the initial apprehension and response of faith – nevertheless the response demanded by his initial apprehension includes an active perseverance in the direction in which this faith points. The powers of the human will are liberated rather than set aside ...[13]

Perseverance then is the note on which this chapter ends. An explicit Christian faith in God and commitment to the Church declines year by year in Western Europe, in England and in the North-East. It may be halted, though the surveys above of the younger generation say exactly the opposite. And there is no escape from the reality of everyday life. Phil Brown pleaded in his study for the Church to be aware of the gulf between the attitudes of many congregations and the attitudes found in ordinary working-class life; Peter Baelz speaks of no magical transformation ignoring the conditions of history. It is the same point made in different circumstances, different ways. The next chapter will look at a theology of the local church and the implications for evangelism. A theology of mission is always a theology of the response of the local church to the call of God and the needs of the area.

CHAPTER 4

Personal Evangelism

He brought light out of darkness, not out of a lesser light; he can bring thy summer out of winter, though thou have no spring; though in the ways of fortune, or understanding, or conscience, thou have been benighted till now, wintered and frozen, clouded and eclipsed, damped and benumbed, smothered and stupefied till now, now God comes to thee, not as in the dawning of the day, not as in the bud of the spring, but as the sun at noon.

> John Donne, "The Light of the World" sermon at St Paul's, 1624

True art discloses "the many-splendoured thing" which we with "our estranged faces" all too easily miss. Thus art can assist the conversion of the imagination which precedes the response of faith. It can open our eyes to see "the many-splendoured thing" which is the refraction of the glory of God in creation and redemption. To this glory the cathedral, I hope and pray, bears a constant and continuing witness.

> Peter Baelz, Durham Cathedral, 1983

The End of Religious Tribalism

Behind Houpeten's analysis of the many forms of modern atheism, and the failure of the Church, there is an underlying emphasis on what he describes as the necessity of "a common search – by all Christians together."[1] This search is for a contemporary belief in God, which sees the Church as the community of the Spirit of God and which lives out their interpretation of Jesus. Not every human desire is a desire for God, and therefore the question for the churches is whether the staggering technological achievements of recent decades, combined with enormous social and cultural changes, have so unnerved them that they no longer feel they have anything to say to modern society. Religion will be listened to not when it is strident but when it can present both a compelling vision of God and a critique of modern society which is critical and yet sympathetic.

The previous two chapters indicate that English society is moving into a world where Christianity is known less and less, and yet this society is not in fact irreligious. The memory of past religious ages lives long in the Church, but is rapidly forgotten elsewhere. A recent study of the High Church Wing of the Church of England, *Catholics in Crisis?*,[2] presented a picture entirely dominated by events of the past. The Christian Socialism of the 1890–1930 period; the founding of the Walsingham Shrine in Norfolk from 1920 to 1970; the work of parish priests in the poverty-stricken areas of the great cities before 1914; the growth of religious communities up to 1968; all this was beautifully conveyed. After that there was only the chronicle of disagreements, decline in numbers and threats of schism. For someone brought up in the High Church world, such as the poet John Betjeman, the communal memory ensured that the anniversaries of great and holy men and women carried on. They were clearly narrated in this study of Anglo-Catholicism as an inspiration for the future. Yet for most people outside the movement, and still more for those outside the churches, all this seems incredible: they echo in half-heard tones as the once proud, now nostalgic memories of a movement where fact and mythology blur together. There is no inspiration here for future generations, however great the past achievements of this movement. This is not to argue that the past cannot speak to us, nor that from within a community already committed to exploring new forms of spirituality such as that of Shepherd's Law the inspiration of particular beliefs and people from the past may not be invaluable. However, in a secular society with a relentless quest for style, novelty and the perfect sexual relationship, the tales of Fr X or Sr Y appear medieval in their remoteness. The gulf between the 1920s and the 1990s is far more than the usual changes over one person's lifetime. It amounts to a social and cultural revolution, although there will be many who will wish to live in the thoughtforms of a previous age.

> Holy Mary, Mother of God
> Pray for me and Tommy Todd
> I'm a Fenian, He's a Prod,
> Holy Mary, Mother of God.

This poem – if you can dignify it with such a description! – is not blasphemous, in fact. It comes from a book describing life in Belfast in the 1920s. Fenians were Roman Catholics, so called from the secret Fenian Society which fought for Irish independence a century ago, and which only recruited Roman Catholics. Prods are of course Protestants. My mother was brought up in Belfast in the 1920s, and my grandmother remembers the children's rhyme. It was common in children's playgrounds. Once, then, your political and culture loyalties were shaped by the religion you outwardly professed. You might not go to church, but you knew who you were: RC or Protestant. Anthony Archer's book *The Two Catholic Churches*[3] describes church life on Tyneside before 1939 in the same way. In the Co. Durham and Yorkshire pit villages it was Church or Chapel. And so one could go on, listing the way in which religion and tribal loyalty ran through streets; jobs in the shipyards; schools and much else. The High Church Movement in the Church of England worked within such tribal groups, building up congregations of great devotion. We live today, however, in a secular society, where the divisions are between haves and have-nots; between those who like the Beasty Boys and those who like Bach; between old and young.

Some of these differences are ones we cannot change: I cannot make myself twenty again, for instance. But others are matters of taste: heavy rock or classical opera. Some still go to church, and most do not, but cultural or social pressures hardly affect people's decision to go these days (it might put them off, of course, as with peer-group pressure on teenagers who belong to a church and are a minority in their class at the local comprehensive). But is the decision to go to church a matter of taste? It is very much my choice, unlike being aged forty, for instance. If we move away from a world of RC or Protestant – and in many areas that is now a memory – what makes us decide to be a church member and a Christian? And are all church members Christian, and vice versa? Personal evangelism in any theology of mission must address the question of how it is possible to speak of God at all, given the total evaporation of communal religious identity for the majority of suburban English society today.

In this chapter, two arguments will be in tension. On the one hand, the credibility of belief in God depends on the attractiveness of the Christian faith in the public world of modern society. Yet it is not simply a community which is appealed to. The community draws its beliefs and values from the objective reality of God, and the activity of God in the world. In this argument contemporary systematic theologians such as Dan Hardy, Stanley Hauerwas and William Vanstone are important, along with church leaders such as John Habgood. However, on the other hand, there are two powerful criticisms of mission by the churches. George Lindbeck believes that the practice of mass evangelism is deeply destructive of Christian identity. Richard Roberts sets the charismatic movement in the Church, and the emphasis on personal awareness, against the socially determined nature of the Church. Both Lindbeck and Roberts believe that the social context of the Church is so compromised that a simple emphasis on evangelism could be destructive of the Church's identity, and lead it further into self-deception. Finally Nicholas Lash offers an interpretation of evangelism related to issues of poverty and deprivation. Yet the two arguments have much in common. Both believe that we live in an age where Christianity is increasingly seen as outmoded and incredible. Both realize that the old structures of authority no longer compel anyone to accept the faith: the "collapse of the house of authority" means that the most important element is that we cannot presume anything in arguing for Christianity, not even that there are certain foundations for belief in God to exist at all. Both finally are concerned with the issue of what it means to speak of God's activity in the world today.

Public Faith

The relationship of public life to religion is the most problematic area in modern Britain. Therefore the 1983 enthronement sermon of John Habgood, Archbishop of York, which is reprinted in his latest book, is bound to touch on an area where agreement is likely to be difficult. Nevertheless John Habgood spells out the religious roots of public life with great clarity.[4] He argues that we live today

> in a country at least partially divided into different religions and cultures; a country conscious of deep social divisions, divisions made even more apparent by our present economic strains; a country with many uncertainties about its aims and values. We have seen the public dimensions of faith steadily eroded.

That analysis has been the major theme of this book as well. How then did the Archbishop resolve to deal with it? He responded by denying that individual faith and goodness should be separated from the foundations of our society. Public faith is about "the things which bind us together, and the values we share, and the goals we pursue". He quoted a verse from Psalm 11, itself written in an uncertain, divided age: "If the foundations are destroyed, what can the just man do?" It was not insignificant that the Prime Minister, in charge of one of the most controversial governments of recent decades, sat impassively in the front rows of York Minster, her face occasionally portrayed on the internal television screens in the Minster.

Yet the Archbishop's argument was far more than a political one. He went on to emphasize how embarrassed people are today to hear a reference to God in ordinary conversation. There is no shortage of highly individualized, often slightly bizarre beliefs, and a reservoir of unrecognzied religious experience. Yet these vague feelings are seldom focused into prayer, commitment and action. Such focusing can only be done with great difficulty in a fragmented society, "so critical, so suspicious of authority".

If that focusing is to take place, two elements must occur, which in fact provide the justification for the two arguments which are in tension in this chapter. On the one hand there is the coherence of the Christian faith, which resists any breaking down into pieces out of context. "To believe only what you like, is to believe only in yourself." The public nature of the faith illuminates the demanding reality of God's presence. Therefore a shared framework of belief allows us to transcend our concern with freedom and choice (again illustrated in the example in the first chapter in the story of Monkseaton). There is the possibility of a judgement of ourselves. Yet a public faith can become complacent and intolerant. Its very coherence leads to self-sufficiency. Furthermore, the Archbishop follows many modern theologians in resisting the ability of a systematically coherent faith to encompass the infinity of God. Hence there is the need for criticism as well, where the static order is overthrown. True faith grows out of this tension.

"Most of us want a comfortable religion, something to take the strain out of living, something to give a respectability to our prejudices." Only ten months separate these words from the previous sermon, but the words are set in a vastly different context. These reflections came from a 1984 local radio broadcast on the miners' strike, given from Radio Newcastle in the midst of much local violence.[5]

> Let the Churches spread around a thin coating of shared values, and then we can all get on with living our own lives... But that is not the way God works ... And God, the disturbing God, asks questions about *us* ... How can those who are deeply divided begin to find a way of reconciliation unless there is an acknowledgement that we are all equally under God's judgement, all equally in need of his forgiveness? Questions on this level do not cut much political ice. Yet one essential reason why the State needs the Church, and why Christians need to be in places where they have to face real political problems, is precisely so that such questions can be asked; and asked in ways which strike home.

Such remarks may not seem to be about personal evangelism. However, the occasions when questions about reconciliation and forgiveness do strike home, irrespective of their political weight, are occasions when the most profound questions might be raised. What does it mean to be human at all? What are the conditions for freedom, responsibility and human hope? What does loving one's neighbour mean in the miners' strike? These are both public and private questions which judge us and lead us on to the possibility of believing in a God Whose actions allow us to be (at our best) free, responsible and loving. In this public discussion there is also the beginning of evangelism: for the Resurrection "is an invitation to live hopefully" in a world where the freedom of God establishes our freedom.[6] Therefore the evocation of God in bitter social struggles is neither vacuous nor pious: it is earthed in the reality of division, yet about the possibility of reconciliation. The alternative is what often happens: social division continues under the surface, slowly eroding a precarious affluence.

The Attractiveness of Christianity

What does it mean for someone to be attractive? It is a quality in sexual relationships which is more obviously recognized than analysed! Yet as well as people who are physically attractive, there are personalities which are repellant and others which attract. By the same argument, there are some institutions and ways of life which are utterly boring and others which compel by their vivacity, warmth and beauty. Belief in God is not usually thought of as being attractive. Yet there is a strand in Christianity going back to St Paul which stresses the truth, goodness and beauty of God. God attracts us by a relationship which involves a change in the person or community involved. Such a change has to do with truth, goodness and beauty.

In Christian tradition, obedience to the truth meant weighing the claims of Christ with intelligent thought; seeking goodness meant being at peace with your neighbour in love and justice, and was not an added extra to belief but was part of it; seeking beauty meant seeing in God the culmination of humanity's search for creativity, art, self-expression and flourishing. God's SHALOM or PLEROMA meant the fullness of truth, of goodness and beauty; the richness or joy of the living God. It is summed up in the Resurrection, the living sign that God's truth, goodness and beauty cannot be overcome. As the American Catholic Bishops wrote in 1983:[7]

> Jesus gives that peace to His disciples, to those who had witnessed the helplessness of the crucifixion and the power of the resurrection (John 20:19, 20, 26). The peace which He gives to them as He greets them as their risen Lord is the fullness of salvation. It is the reconciliation of the world of

God (Romans 5:1-2; Colossians 1:20); the restoration of the unity and harmony of all creation which the Old Testament spoke of with such longing. Because the walls of hostility between God and humankind were broken down in the life and death of the true, perfect servant, union and well-being between God and the world were finally possible (Ephesians 2:13-22; Galatians 3:28). As His first gift to His followers, the risen Jesus gave his gift of peace. This gift permeated the meetings between the risen Jesus and His followers (John 20:19-29). Simultaneously Jesus gave His Spirit to those who followed Him. These two personal and communal gifts are inseparable. In the Spirit of Jesus the community of believers was enabled to recognise and to proclaim the Saviour of the world.

What is set out here is the claim that belief in God is a response to God's gift of truth, goodness and beauty. *Truth* in the claims of Christ about His Resurrection; *goodness* in the peace which He brings; *beauty* in the restoration of harmony to creation. Belief is a response to all this, and a living from it. It is not just a matter of truth about certain biblical passages. That impoverishes belief greatly. We share in God, because God shares in us, and belief is precisely not a matter of taste or choice, but a sharing in God because God affirms us as people who matter to God. That is our basic worth, and our basic message.

Christians do not in fact believe "in the Bible" or "in doctrine". Bible and doctrine are rather means by which we come to know the presence of God, and share as a congregation in God's truth, goodness and beauty. So Scripture and doctrine need to be taken into the world of prayer and daily experience, and become part of our response to God. Scripture becomes part of our response as we share it with others, and read it and relate it to stories about our daily life. Events from our daily life will resonate with Scripture. Religious belief has a stability about it built up by years of responding to God, grappling with the truth and demonstrating it to others. Religious belief is a way of speaking about long-term judgements about how truth, goodness and beauty are found in our world. They are found because we see God as the reason why the basic conditions of human life are the way they are. We see God as affirming the world, and through this world which God creates, sustains, gives meaning to, and gives an end and a hope to, we come to know God in Himself: the glory of God in the face of Jesus Christ. But we come to know God only in and through our daily life which has the life, energy, peace and order it has from God. The Gospel is "God with us".

One of the most powerful recent restatements of the need for mission has also been most critical of past attempts at mission, which is a tension repeatedly echoed in this book as well. *Jubilate – Theology in Praise* by Dan Hardy and David Ford tells of mission as often proceeding "from doubtful motives" and being carried out badly and insensitively.[8] Yet the authors go on to criticize even further: it is not that mission has been crudely performed, although the concept is basically sound. It is not just a perversion of the good. Much more, many of the contemporary concepts of mission are deeply questionable. What is questionable here is the familiar functional concept of mission: it fills gaps in your life, it repairs what has gone wrong, it is practical in a host of ways. Yet the Gospel is only attractive if Christianity is seen as the abundant generosity of God beyond all human need. God is there in the world anyway. The abundance of God is poured out on the world beyond any conscious mission. But where the activity of God is taken up and recognized in its sheer attractiveness, a community based on the intrinsic worth, beauty and love of God can begin to emerge.

It is clear that the Church often falls far, far short of this.

The irony of the moralizing of Christianity is that it does not even let us live in accordance with the morality. The tragedy of it is that it takes the joy out of goodness. Generations of "good" people in the West have had their Christianity made dull and impotent by moralism.[9]

Christianity is reduced to moral principles, and even in a society such as Victorian England, with its class divisions and tribal barriers, what was often stressed as the one theory which mattered was living in harmony with moral principles. It is easy to mock at this: a liberal indifference to moral constraints may be no more than a reflection of a half-secular society. Yet the pervasion of daily life with notions of worth and status, finely graded according to wealth and achievement, destroys the possibility of simply living according to moral principles.[10] The free respect given by one person to another is possible only when there is a dynamic empowering that respect and challenging networks of esteem. The claim of Christianity is that at its best it can create communities who are based on the present reality of God. Therefore now relationships of self-worth not based on status are possible.

Thus mission is not about meeting needs or filling gaps. That is deeply manipulative evangelism, and people are quite correct to reject it, however sincere the evangelist may be. Mission is about the attractiveness of God, and the creation of a community in which trust, worth and value are possible. Such a community cannot be self-contained. It will spill over into the world. The horizons of that community are set not by the constraints of society, but by God. The goal of history is the activity of God: theologically this is called God's Kingdom, which was the message preached by Jesus, as discussed on p. 00. Equally such a community will need to use the insights of psychology to avoid self-deception. Again the moralism of Christianity plays clean against this: in a situation where keeping moral principles is seen as achieving a harmonious relationship with God and one's neighbour, psychology can destroy the logic of the whole edifice.

What sort of community might a renewed understanding of mission spring from? The whole thrust of this book is that as mission must be worked out in the local context, so too must community. Yet two general descriptions might be mentioned, from very different perspectives.

The Response to God

Mission must be centred in contemporary reality, affirming the day-to-day relationships of ordinary people. It can look to neither past glories, nor to an assumption that mission will fill a need. One version is set in the past, while the other is only one more version of manipulative salesmanship. Instead mission begins with the attractiveness of God, present and praised in the community of those who recognize His reality. What community might this be?

William Vanstone is a High Church Anglican, who worked for over thirty years on a council estate in the North of England. Vanstone's book, *Love's Endeavour, Love's Expense*, which is his reflection on that experience, has had an effect on students whom I have known like no other book I have come across. The searing quality of its writing is based on the sheer commitment of the author to the value of God's love in the most boring, mundane reality. Stanley Hauerwas's *The Peaceable Kingdom* is an attempt by an American Evangelical Methodist from Texas to write an account of a community which puts integrity and trust at its heart. The context is America after the trauma of Vietnam, where violence and power seem a routine part of government. The book is, in the author's words, neither Catholic nor Protestant.

Vanstone sees the lack of the Church as embodying a response to the love of God. There is no general pattern of response by human beings to God. In particular, in concrete situations the love of God is seen as taking risks, failing and needing redress, succeeding and building on that success. In such particular events God works to build up individuals and groups. Vanstone is utterly sceptical of talk of "the fulfilment of humanity" or "the emergence of persons as persons". There is only x or y in his or her own time and place. God seeks our response to His love in that particularity. Yet God's love does not compel our response. It waits upon a response "in which its own nature and quality is understood".[11] Such a response is itself a form of creativity, of understanding, of a new way of being in the world. "The offering is the coming-to-be of understanding: only where this understanding has come to be has love conveyed its richest blessing and completed its work in triumph."[12] Without that understanding, love issues in tragedy. So again and again Vanstone sees love scorned, ignored, and the humdrum existence of daily life becoming a tragic dissolution of God's purposes of love. Conversely recognition of love is not a psychological state of mind, but a creative celebration: "That by which or in which, the love of God is celebrated may be called 'the Church'."[13] However, such a definition takes the Church wider than any ecclesiastical body. Therefore it includes any action done out of awareness of God's love and the private meditation which articulates such awareness. Creative activity will result in structure and form, and so an institution will come into being. However that institution will be subject to change, expressing its willingness to be dynamic and to struggle for its true existence. The Church articulates the response of creation in complete freedom to the love of God. Such divine love is vulnerable, waiting, precarious and totally self-giving. It is like the complete exhaustion of a person of enormous gifts who devotes his or her entire energy to the rescuing of an otherwise impossible situation.[14]

Thus the Church invites others to join it in responding to that love of God. It is "an offering fashioned by discipline out of freedom".[15] It is done because love without that response has elicited nothing. Can this be of any value in personal evangelism? This is not evangelism as meeting human need, but as an invitation to join in transcending oneself in celebrating the meaning, purpose and worth of life, which is the complete self-giving of God in and through all structures, institutions and created life. Such an inspiration may also confer stability, identity and community on a local community. But these benefits are not the reason why the Church exists. With years of experience Vanstone spells out the social value of the Church in our complex world: it is a small-scale, locally based, flexible agency of social care, and such decentralized bodies are now much in favour. All of this Vanstone is able to commend: "the possession of these qualities may enable the Church to exert a social influence much greater than its resources of manpower, money and expertise would suggest."[16] Yet this is not the ultimate value of the Church. The Church is there to recognize God's ever-venturing love, which is a love always on the brink of failure. In a memorable image, Vanstone speaks of the God whom he worships as like a face discovered under a pile of rubbish: a living face buried by the tragedies of creation, which he struggles to bear and carry away.[17]

Therefore the primary task for the Church as a community must be the praise of God. This is taken up in a recent ecumenical report by Anglicans and Lutherans, *The Niagara Report*. The Church praises God as a people claimed by God to proclaim the triumphs of God's love. The Church praises God as Trinity in order that it may be shaped and grasped by that God for its life. In all it does the Church receives with thanksgiving the establishing of God's promises on earth.

If this is not an attractive prospect for the world, then the Church must accept this fact. There is always the need for the Church to express more fully its struggle and commitment. This search is so that we may respond in creative freedom to the love of God which is no pre-ordained programme. The love of God often suffers our rebuff. Nevertheless our response is the deepest self-offering of ourselves which we can make. This is again echoed in the *Niagara Report*, which states:

> All powers and dominions in this age believe, in the last analysis, that death has the last word. The appropriate expres-

sion of such belief is humanity's unrelenting drive for self-preservation. But if the Christ has the last word, then the appropriate expression is rather self-offering, confident in the knowledge that there is more to do with life than preserve it. Those who seek to save their lives will lose them anyway. But those who offer their lives for Christ's sake will find their true selves, will find life itself (Matthew 16:24–26). The apostolicity of the Church is the mission of self-offering (not self-preservation) for the life of the world. The Church to be thus serves the reign of God, not the reign of death. The Church serves the mission of God's suffering and vulnerable love, not a mission of its own devising. The Church serves the mission grounded in and shaped by Christ's way of being in the world.[18]

It is therefore fundamental to Vanstone that what goes on in church life may be trivial, the building will be maintained by people good with their hands anyway, and music will be performed by those whose hobby it is. People will use the Church as one more expression of their hobbies, and it will also be a place (as Phil Brown's friend said) of conflict and disagreement. Vanstone does not deny any of this. Nor is it to be at all covered up that for many, perhaps most, people the Church is quite irrelevant in their prosperous, busy lives. What matters is that there is a reality which we call God, and who gives all creation meaning, purpose and value in all the tragedies and opportunities of daily life. This action is enormously costly to God: it is not an easy Lordship over the world. What matters also is that somewhere this self-giving of God should be recognized and praised. It is this task, which is a task of establishing and living from goodness, truth and beauty, which the Church calls people to be part of. It is no part of that call to deny that in that response to God people will perhaps quite regularly use the Church as one more hobby for their own activities. It is always to be resisted, for such use can confine the struggle of the Church for free praise of God's love into the suburban domesticity of the comfortably respectable. Nevertheless at its best such offering of particular gifts can become a costly self-offering of all which we have. Personal evangelism in Vanstone's ministry will involve leading people on from where they are in particular settings to having a vision of their life as a response to God. Particular settings include the children who patiently create a model of a waterfall; a foster-parent to a family of children; a nurse caring for the long-term mentally ill patients inside a hospital. All these disciplined acts of caring can be taken up into the offering of the Church. It is however crucial to realize that for Vanstone there will always be two different awarenesses of God's love. On the one hand there is the beauty of creation, relationships, art and truth; the attractiveness of Christianity. What is much less obviously responded to is the hiddenness of God's love. It is this which personal evangelism is finally about. In the well-known words of Vanstone's prayer at the end of his book, which are now set to music as a hymn:

> Open, Lord, are these thy gifts
> Gifts of love, to mind and sense;
> Hidden is love's agony,
> Love's endeavour, Love's expense.
>
> Drained is love in making full;
> Bound in setting others free;
> Poor in making many rich;
> Weak in giving power to be.[19]

We turn to the other description of mission as centred upon a community set in the contemporary reality of the world and yet expressing the relationship of God and the world. Hauerwas's argument echoes Vanstone at many points. Again there is the insistence that it is the empirical Church which matters. No mystical community is more real than "the concrete church with parking lots and potluck dinners". "The church is not just a 'community' but an institution that has budgets, buildings, pot luck dinners, heated debates about who should be the next pastor, and so on."[20] Again the Church exists to show the world what the reality of God is like. Yet this is not ignoring the world. Like Vanstone, Hauerwas defines the world as that place where God's goodness is set forth, and it is a world created by the goodness of God. Thus Church and world are relational concepts: the world is where in freedom we choose not yet to believe in God, and cherish the illusion that we control the nature of our lives. Yet, as Hauerwas argues, the only way we control our lives with any security is by manipulation, violence and lack of trust. Thus Hauerwas takes one step beyond Vanstone, although it is only a logical implication of Vanstone's argument. "Our task is the demanding one of trying to understand rightly the world as world . . . the first question we must ask is not 'what should we do' but 'what is going on?'"[21]

Therefore the Church can never abandon the world to a state of hopelessness. Personal evangelism turns on the Church being "a people with a hope sufficiently fervid to sustain the world as well as itself". If Vanstone's vision could serve as a background to Shepherd's Law, Hauerwas's could relate to the group discussing the Star Centre or the North Kenton project. The Church therefore exists to tell the stories of Israel and Jesus. The Church lives in such a way as to make the Kingdom visible. It is not the Kingdom of God, but it manifests it as a foretaste of it. Thus for Hauerwas everything turns on whether a particular community can in each generation speak out the story of God. "You cannot tell the story of God without including within it the story of Israel and the church."[22] Scripture is an aspect of the community's self-understanding. Equally the community exists only because of the faithfulness of God. Belief in the Church means belief in the calling of people by God, who sustains them in their life. But how does the Church show the world a sign of hope, and how does it listen truthfully to the story of God in the very act of its telling of that story? Here the issues of self-deception, old class antagonisms and lack of integrity press home.

Hauerwas therefore replies that the way to listen truthfully, be a sign of hope, and proclaim the story of God is to be a particular kind of people. There are obvious dangers here, for which he has been repeatedly and stringently criticized. Is this not a retreat to a "reservation of the human spirit", as the American Indians live on their reservations? Is this not the final abandonment of the Church in daily life, where people are forced to compromise and nothing is straightforward? Does it not lead to pure sectarianism, where the devout conscience proclaims its innocence of the world's guilt to those who listen (if any)? However, Haeruwas's reply is that he does not advocate "a withdrawal ethic; nor is it a self-righteous attempt to flee from the world's problems".[23] Instead it is an attempt to live a life without coercion, lies and falsehood. Again this can rightly lead to further criticisms of hypocrisy. So, as in Vanstone's argument, the Church is committed to a struggle and an arduous task. "We are required to be patient and never lose hope." The struggle is to be a people without coercion and with integrity. Baptism takes members of the Church into the story of God's people; Eucharist or communion shows the living reality of God's presence and peace in the world. Hauerwas argues that this entails trying to live without fear. He takes an illustration from the Masai people, whose exchange of grass was not a sign of peace, but was peace.[24]

There are strong social implications of Hauerwas's position in seeking justice and peace. Yet this chapter is about evangelism. "Joy is the result of our letting go of the slim reed of security that we think provides us with the power to control our own and others' lives."[25] We need to learn the skills to set aside our own illusions. Insofar as a community can live that way, without control, joyful in the face of the tragic, it has something to offer. Like Vanstone, Hauerwas is deeply aware of the all-pervasive world of the secular, with its rejection of talk of the divine, of religion, of the reality of God. Like Vanstone's work, *The*

Peaceable Kingdom is about the formation of a community which can live without control. Such communities are about spirituality, and about being a community of trust. They are firmly set in the contemporary world, and while inspired by history they are not entrapped in a cultural time-lag. They are immersed in social involvement, yet their ultimate vindication is only the invisible reality which they seek to respond to. It is in the sustaining of these communities that denominations may keep some hope of belief in God alive in our society. They are the local church, set in the context of a North of England housing estate, or the suburban reality of an American nation in the years after Vietnam and Watergate, Irangate and Ivan Boesky. Such local communities are the expression of, and the presupposition for, a theology of mission in the liberal post-Christian world in which we now live. It is in the theology of Vanstone and Hauerwas that we see the justification of a theology of mission based on the local church in its neighbourhood. This theology is undergirded by the development of a belief in God as fundamentally the most attractive reality there is in society, and by a commitment to a faith publicly expressed.

A Criticism of Mass Evangelism

The position worked out in the preceding pages is a defence of the attractiveness of Christianity and a vindication of the local church as the primary agent in mission. This leaves two questions unanswered, however. What efforts should the Church make to evangelize Israel? Secondly, should the Church seek to grow as fast as possible? The answer to these questions has been hotly debated by many writers on mission, and there is an influential "Church Growth" movement. In an attempt to explore these issues, George Lindbeck, an American Lutheran theologian, uses the analysis of narrative or story-telling. George Lindbeck sees the Church's story as continuous with Israel's. God chooses a people to be a sign of and witness to Who and What God is. Whether it acts obediently or not, it is that witness. It is in the life of this people that the mercy and judgement of God are manifest, as nowhere else.[26]

Lindbeck defends this claim by arguing that early Christian communal self-understanding was shaped by story or narrative. The story came first.[27] Only after the story had been told could images such as "the body of Christ" or the marks of the Church be understood. (Indeed, in Chapter 1 this method has been followed. The story of the Star Centre, and what it means as a sign of hope, was told before the marks of the Church were explored. "One, holy, catholic and apostolic" are marks of the Church as a statement of hope and faith, but there must be a sign of hope and a community whose story of faith can be told before these marks can be understood.) It is not that images, concepts and theories of the Church are first understood by learning theology, and then applied to the life of the Church. Rather the story of particular churches determines the use of images and concepts, although these are not to be therefore devalued in an attack on traditional theology. So "the Church" refers primarily to a concrete community, not to an invisible idea. That community as Christian theology began was the early Church, and it looked back to the history of Israel as its history. It was the whole of this history which it studied, including stories of the rebelliousness and wickedness of Israel. The story of Israel is by no means entirely happy: often it is deeply tragic. The Old Testament can often be read as a tragic work. Yet even when the judgement of God falls on Israel, Lindbeck argues that Paul believes in the faithfulness of God. The identity of the people of God, who live by the promises of God, remains the same. "The gifts and the call of God are irrevocable" (Romans 11:29).[28] Judaism remains part of one overarching story, and unbelieving Israel will be restored at the end of time.

If this is so, Lindbeck believes that the fundamental issue is the identity of the Church. The identity of the Church rests on the choice of God, not on its faithfulness. Secondly, the sacraments are both blessing and curse, depending on how they are received. Thirdly, election is a corporate communal action. Individuals belong to Christ by virtue of being part of a visible memebership of the Church. Finally, the primary mission of the Church is to witness to God, who judges and saves, not to save those who (as some still argue today) would not be saved if the Church did not reach out to them.

Lindbeck makes the whole nature of mission turn on the communal identity of the Church. As he rightly says, this amounts to a revolutionary understanding of evangelization, and one which must be controversial. He writes in uncompromising tones:

> Also Jewish sounding is the Church's mission. It is above all by the character of its communal life that it witnesses, that it proclaims the gospel and serves the world. This revolutionizes one traditional understanding of proclamation of evangelism. While it is crucial that all kinds of human beings – Greek, barbarian, female and slave as well as Jew, male and free – be fully part of the community, sheer numbers are, at most, of tertiary importance.[29]

Why does Lindbeck argue in this way? In a secular, or quasi-secular, society a viewpoint that numbers does not matter very much will strike many Evangelical Christians as selling the path totally. Yet Lindbeck is not arguing this from a position that the only Gospel which matters is social justice. Indeed, he explicitly denies this: "It would be a mistake, however, to conclude from this in the currently popular fashion that the church's mission is primarily diakonia in the sense of serving the needs of humanity at large."[30] If Lindbeck is interested in neither Church growth nor social justice as the main emphasis of mission, his position will seem odd, not to say eccentric, for many concerned to increase the Church's interest in mission. Why does Lindbeck, who is one of the most prominent North American theologians currently writing, argue this way?

Lindbeck distinguishes between different social contexts of mission. Where there are many who are basically Christian in their socio-religious identity, the attempt to bring them back to Church membership can be seen as a call for the unfaithful to become (once more?) faithful. This is of course the standard technique of Protestant revivalism, such as that practised by John Wesley or Jonathan Edwards. Lindbeck has no disagreement with this, "however questionable some of the techniques".[31] A second social context is that of mass conversions. This repeatedly occurred in Northern Europe after Constantine became a Christian emperor. It also occurred on many occasions in Africa, Asia and South America. Lindbeck sees this as the collapse of one socio-religious identity (the old religion and culture) and the entry into a new one. The response of the early Church, through leaders such as Ambrose of Milan and Cyril of Jerusalem, was to insist on a prolonged education for those seeking entry. "Yet such devices have repeatedly failed, and whole societies have become nominally Christian, with the result that membership becomes easy, almost automatic and totally comprehensive." The defence of this strategy is that there is salvation only within the Church, or that the hearing of the Gospel message is imperative for salvation and this is unlikely to be heard outside the Church community. But, Lindbeck says,

> Whatever the merits of such reasoning when Christendom is intact, it invites disaster when Christendom fades. The churches now increasingly consist of people who have been culturally and linguistically dechristianised and yet retain a residual attachment to the ancestral faith. Return to stricter standards of membership seems imperative if distinctively Christian identity is to be maintained, but this means abandoning the notion that it is the church's business to entice as many as possible.[32]

It is crucial to Lindbeck's argument that "identity" is the key to the meaning of Christianity. Where someone has lost touch with any Christian identity, Lindbeck claims that it is in the long run of no help to that person or the Church to bring them into the Christian community unless he or she knows what that involves. Therefore Lindbeck relies on the sociological fact that, in his words, "many individuals are socially alienated or unlocated".[33] So a mission strategy which tries to make churches grow as fast as possible is one which Lindbeck rejects. The implications for many forms of mass evangelism are obvious.

He claims that

> The Bible gives us no warrants for saying that all those who do not become Christians are, in any case, excluded from the coming Kingdom, although it cannot be said of them as of Christians that salvation, the Kingdom, is already present among or in them (Luke 17:21). The purpose of that presence of salvation, furthermore, is witness, and it is up to God to add whom He will to the company (Acts 2:47) ... The primary Christian mission, in short is not to save souls but to be a faithfully witnessing people.[34]

There is in this argument a theological presupposition that religion does not spring from personal experience. Again this is likely to be deeply controversial. Religion is seen neither as a symbolism expressive of basic attitudes, feelings and attitudes (which is the typical Evangelical definition of religion, where music, prayers and testimonies convey the inner experience of "meeting with Jesus") nor as a set of statements about the way the world is, and what is good. Instead religion is like a culture or language, which is a communal phenomenon.[35] Like learning French, as my ten-year-old son is, it makes it possible to understand how other people live: it is a way into a whole culture of different experiences, feelings and beliefs. Thus the journey to France to stay with a family is an integral part of learning French, not a luxurious extra. The culture shapes the experiences of individuals, rather than the other way round. Within that culture feelings and beliefs will be generated, and beliefs about how the world is will be stated. Yet the primary emphasis must always be on religion as a way of life which structures "human experience and understanding of self and world". Religion is not different from other cultural forms of life. While it is true that religions change, this is not from new experiences. The changes result from the interaction of a religion with new situations. This produces negative effects and experiences, which religion cannot cope with; prophetic figures point out the contradictions in the situation, and how the religious tradition must change.

Yet Lindbeck writes this with a deep pessimism. He knows all too well that the rationalization, mobility and pluralism of modern life dissolves the patterns of community and tradition: "This produces multitudes of men and women who are impelled, if they have religious yearnings, to embark on their own individual quest for symbols of transcendence.[36] The churches have responded to purveying individual salvation, in mystical, liberal or charismatic forms. Mystics search for an inner peace and harmony with God, sometimes allied with Jungian doctrines of the anima or soul; liberals seek personal wholeness, with a holistic lifestyle, which is socially aware, as exemplified in Don Cupitt's writings and broadcasts;[37] charismatics find personal release in ecstatic religious experience and a meeting with the Lord.[38] However, the fundamental Biblical understanding of religion is of a communal people who encounter God in their journey through history. While there is much debate within this community, there is also a coherent outlook on life. However, as Lindbeck says, in modern society selfhood is seen as prior to social influences: the myth of the transcendental (or invulnerable) ego. "Fulfilment comes [in our society] from . . . penetrating into the inner depths rather than from communally responsible action in the public world."

Yet the culture which is so hostile to what Lindbeck calls

"post-liberalism", or an account of religion which goes beyond the liberal's concern with feelings and "how-is-it-with-you?", paradoxically needs religion more than ever if society is to survive at all.

> Similarly, the viability of a unified world of the future may well depend on counteracting the acids of modernity. It may depend on communal enclaves that socialise their members into highly particular outlooks supportive of concern for others rather than for personal fulfilment. It is at least an open question whether any religion will have the requisite toughness for this demanding task unless it at some point makes the claim that it is significantly different and unsurpassably true ... Thus it may well be that post-liberal theologies are more applicable than liberal ones to the needs of the future.[39]

It would be easy to caricature Lindbeck's criticism of "mission as mass evangelism". It can be seen as perverse, intellectually superior and culturally élitist. Yet Lindbeck does not disagree with evangelism. Rather he is concerned with the question of whether those who enter the Church have realized what it is they take on. Many parish clergy will have countless requests for baptism, and have many casual adherents who occasionally attend church. Again Lindbeck, as I understand him, is not seeking to exclude such requests. There are many parts of rural England where Christian identity is still well understood by those who choose not to attend church and worship; the reasons for this lie deep in the history of their community. Lindbeck writes from an entirely urban, cosmopolitan culture. It is true that churchgoing is much higher in the United States than here, but it is also true that there are large aspects of modern life which appear entirely without an understanding of Christianity. Chapters 2 and 3 of this book have sought to demonstrate this point. The task for the churches is not to reject those who seek after truth, or are half-believers, whose religion is "a forgotten dream". Instead the churches should seek to be as open as possible, while preserving their own identity.

Equally in the area of social witness and action Lindbeck argues that all human beings are called to a "commitment to peace, justice and freedom".[40] The Church's task is to preserve its own integrity and so be "a liberating force in world history". Here I feel Lindbeck ignores the de-humanizing effect of much modern society upon the poor and unskilled. This reads to me like a theological version of the trickle-down wealth theory, where the benefits of the rich creating yet more wealth will trickle down to the rest of society. I cannot believe that the "liberation of the world" will happen unless the powerful forces creating wider divisions in society are counterbalanced. In this the Church must have a role to play alongside many other agencies. Nevertheless, Lindbeck's criticism of a Church which is more concerned with every worldwide instance of social unrest and suffering than the building up of the faith is a justifiable corrective against pure activism. The Church has no future if it is one more agency for human well-being: "when serving the world results in the neglect of the household of faith, the church becomes not a sign but a countersign, a contributor to that human confusion which is the opposite of God's design."[41]

What is the implication of this criticism? Lindbeck warns against "the arrogant self-righteousness of the company of the visibly holy",[42] a warning which should be stamped on every book on mission, like a government health warning. Lindbeck's argument leads to the importance of the local Christian church community, which knows what it is about and tries to build up its brothers and sisters by means of worship, teaching, social involvement and community life. It is through the mission of the local church, and not "the electronic vulgarity of television evangelists" that we shall come to know God.[43] However important the place of personal experience of God, for many men and women, such experience has to be set within a community or way of life. A purely personal relationship with God is in the end of the day no more authentic than visiting a supermarket with French flags over bottles of French wine and accordion music is an experience of French daily life. Yet the churches would do well to avoid over-judgemental remarks about personal religion. Their credibility is low in modern society, and the disappearance of religion from the daily life of many people ensures that the religious quest will be fragmented and confused. All the examples cited in the first chapter bear this out explicitly. What does seem to be ruled out on Lindbeck's analysis is any mass evangelism by a popular evangelist, either in person or on television, unless it is followed by prolonged education at a local church. This invites the comment that one may as well start there anyway. Thus Lindbeck's analysis is actually one of great comfort to the local congregation, so long as that openness to the world is in fact there. It is by the witness of a local community that God is to be found in the confusions of modern society, and not in the strident voices of the sophisticated, modern mass evangelism with its doubtful appeal to feelings of guilt and despair in the individual. The Church's story is itself a witness to the faithfulness of God, and it is in the living of that story in the local community that witness will go on.

Another criticism is made by Richard Roberts, where he criticizes Simon Tugwell's *Did you Receive the Spirit?* and J. V. Taylor's *The Go-Between God*.[44] Richard Roberts argues that Tugwell's work is marked by "a fundamental disrespect for the complexity of human social, moral, emotional and aesthetic life . . . a posture of uncritical passivity". Tugwell seeks to reunite "spirituality and dogma", but the "letting go into God" which is advocated becomes entirely individualist and unaware of the society in which the person is set. Tugwell realizes that the release of the unconscious by the Spirit may involve deep tensions, but he believes that "the truly spiritual man can let God be God". Richard Roberts comments:

> The contingency of the social world is "short-circuited" in the spasmodic resolution of religious experience . . . the evasion of intrinsic complexity in the order of social reality by sudden and arbitrary resolution of the human into a unified divine given in a supra-historical reconciliation.[45]

Equally Bishop Taylor's invocation of the Holy Spirit is also criticized for allowing timeless resolutions in the face of social reality. Taylor applies too easily the emotional enlightenment of the individual Christian, enhanced by an awareness of the Spirit, to the problems facing those who are socially constrained by their position. Again it is worth quoting Richard Roberts briefly:

> Affirmation and negation are inseparable and the Church will only understand its own existence when it knows that it is simultaneously bound by the social determination of its consciousness and yet free to commit itself to obedience in faith by the power of its Trinitarian being.[46]

Conclusion

What is needed therefore is for the communal vision offered by Vanstone and Hauerwas to be earthed in a particular social reality, as Vanstone hints in his book. As Nicholas Lash writes, there are constants in discipleship, but there are no timelessly appropriate answers. What fidelity to the Gospel requires can be decided only in the light of particular concrete circumstances.

Lash remarks that the Brazilian Dominican theologian Frei Betto gave an unexpected answer to the question "What should Europe free itself from?" His reply was that he was a liberation theologian, and there were many poor, unemployed people in London, Liverpool, Manchester, etc. But the greatest challenge to the Church was the lack of belief in this country. It was, he said, a "pagan nation". Betto linked evangelization to the

Church's commitment to the poor. If the Gospel announces God's relationship with his people in friendship and love, then there must also be the promise and necessity of relationship between people. Relationships involve community, and Christianity "is about the gift, and fact, and promise of community."[47] Therefore Lash pleads for an attempt to discern

> in common prayer and practical reflection – ways of discerning the connections between eucharist and fraternity, between faith and politics, between the quest for earthly justice and the peace which only God can give.

Finally, Lash believes that a deeper commitment by the churches to those who are poor in Britain would have to avoid patronage at all costs. Yet there is much to gain from the poor. He notes astutely that in contemporary Britain there is much material prosperity, but little joy.

> Ask any visitor from overseas what strikes them most . . . you will not hear mention of joy, gentleness or hospitality. These things are more securely stifled by egotism than by poverty and, though the rest of us have no right to them we are, as Christians, perhaps entitled to pray that we might receive these gifts, for our redemption, from Christ's poor.

The echo of Patrick Cotton's remarks in Fawdon about the richness of inner-city life is quite striking. At the end of the November 1982 conference in Newcastle Civic Centre on co-operation between Church and city, one of the participants noted in a report that the question of the inability of most Christians to articulate their faith was as pressing as the social action which the Church was struggling to carry out. She noted, however, that it was a problem which was passed over in the conference, despite its place in the Bishop of Newcastle's address. He argued that the weakness of the Church was that its members tended to be either totally absorbed into what was going on, or "so separate that they are never defiled at all". There was a need for the Church to go on being in dialogue with those in public life about their values and goals, and to seek to assist by many practical projects in deprived areas. There was also an overriding need "to make more people Christian and more people more Christian". If that did not happen, there was no future for the Church, and no hope for secular society. For secular society, as Jeremy Beecham, Leader of the City Council, said in his address to the conference, was complex and pluralist today. There was a deep challenge to the future of the city in the hopelessness of those who were unemployed and poor. The answer must be a dialogue of Church and city:

> Church and city must listen to those who participate in the affairs of each and the voices of those who do not seek actively to play a part in either; and we must listen to each other for our different but shared experiences surely form two of the essential ingredients in the evaluation of the sense of purpose and of community which alone will lead to the building in Newcastle of a just city.[48]

There is then, for the Church, no dichotomy between evangelism which is sensitive to where others are, and playing a deeply involved part in the social concerns of the modern city. "Now with our own particular viewpoint, derived from light shed by Christ's cross, we seek with secular society a solution to the world's intractable problems." The remarks of Alec Graham, Bishop of Newcastle, are embodied in the local church as it responds to the pressing reality of the love of God, and lives out its life as a community of the Kingdom. Such a community will always be flawed, but insofar as it is true to its calling, the life of the local church which listens to the needs of the local community will be in itself evangelism: a proclamation of the good news of God for this community. The current life of the Church is the most eloquent apologia for the reality of God's love, even if this study has repeatedly showed how this life can be broken by the reality of human ignorance and frailty. In the words of one of the most important recent ecumenical documents, *Baptism, Eucharist and Ministry*:[49]

> In a broken world God calls the whole of humanity to become God's people. For this purpose God chose Israel, and then spoke in a unique and decisive way in Jesus Christ, God's Son. Jesus made his own the nature, condition and cause of the whole human race, giving himself as a sacrifice for all. Jesus' life of service, his death and resurrection, are the foundation of a new community which is built up continually by the good news of the Gospel and the gifts of the sacrament. The Holy Spirit unites in a single body those who follow Jesus Christ and sends them as witnesses into the world. Belonging to the Church means living in communion with God through Jesus Christ in the Holy Spirit.
>
> The life of the Church is based on Christ's victory over the powers of evil and death, accomplished once for all. Christ offers forgiveness, invites to repentance and delivers from destruction. Through Christ, people are enabled to turn in praise to God and in service to their neighbours. In Christ they find the source of new life in freedom, mutual forgiveness and love. Through Christ their hearts and minds are directed to the consummation of the Kingdom where Christ's victory will become manifest and all things made new. God's purpose is that, in Jesus Christ all people should share in this fellowship.

CHAPTER 5

Industrial Mission

I journeyed to London, to the timekept City,
Where the River flows, with foreign flotations.
There I was told: we have too many churches,
And too few chop-houses. There I was told:
Let the vicars retire. Men do not need the Church
In the place where they work,
   but where they spend their Sundays.
In the City, we need no bells:
Let them waken the suburbs.
I journeyed to the suburbs, and there I was told:
We toil for six days, on the seventh we must motor
To Hindhead or Maidenhead.
If the weather is foul
   we stay at home and read the papers.

When your fathers fixed the place of GOD,
And settled all the inconvenient saints,
Apostles, martyrs, in a kind of Whipsnade,
Then they could set about imperial expansion
Accompanied by industrial development.
Exporting iron, coal and cotton goods
And intellectual enlightenment
And everything, including capital
And several versions of the Word of GOD:
The British race assured of a mission
Performed it, but left much at home unsure.

T. S. Eliot, *The Rock*

The Closure of Consett

In his account of the closure of the British Steel plant at Consett, Co. Durham, from December 1979 to December 1980, the industrial chaplain at the works, John Eyles, comments critically on how the closure took place.[1]

> Right at the start the pattern seemed to be set for all that followed. Confusion and uncertainty appeared to predominate, combined at times with rushed action of great swiftness ... The response [to the closure announcement] of the first few days turned Consett into a cauldron of emotions and reactions of every kind – individuals experienced anger, disbelief and a wide variety of physical symptoms of ill health. Different union groups expressed all out resistance to closure seen as a betrayal of efforts of the recent past, or proposed acceptance of closure with hard bargaining over terms, and active promotion of Consett and its people as a good place for new industry.

The General Manager was moved overnight four days before the closure announcement. Although the works had just moved into slight profit and record-breaking performances, these changes had come too late to save Consett. There was no negotiation offered on the decision to close the plant. What was worse, the steelworks became caught up in a national strike which no one locally wanted. So the Iron and Steel Union was able to call a strike nationally about pay without a ballot and the local unions drifted into it, unsure as to whether they had joined the strike or been laid off. Thus it was not until March 1980 that demonstrations to save the plant took place, while the strike dragged on. They were good-humoured demonstrations: thousands took part across the town, involving workers and local people. It was the only major industry employing over 3,000 men.

The strike ended in April and production records were again

broken at the plant. However, there was no date given for the closure. Therefore speculation and unease grew.

> Neither work nor private life could be planned in the face of such total uncertainty. Many people, perhaps a very large majority, wanted the works to remain open, but they wanted an open future, not a day to day existence. Closure was preferable to that.

By June the date for closure was announced, with the reasons for closure. The works would close at the end of September, because the decline in the motor industry and in engineering had drastically cut demand. This more or less broke the workforce. There was an immediate response eight days later of a mass meeting of 3,000 employees, which sought to avert the closure by a plan to move the works into producing more sophisticated products. Yet management dismissed these plans, and the unions themselves were slow to publish details. There was a much-publicized march in London to Parliament, but it was noteworthy that it was quite hard to fill the train from Consett. Was it, some wondered, just a political event? The unions set their minds on negotiating alternative plans for the works, but increasingly their strategy was doubted in Consett itself. A second march across Consett at the end of July was an anticlimax. Few attended at all. Instead redundancy counselling began in earnest at a frantic pace from mid-July. It continued throughout August, despite union opposition. Most people sought information about retraining and payments. Later this counselling was described as inadequate, but it was probably the best available.

The end finally came after 29 August 1980. The management of British Steel nationally, including the Chairman, met and rejected the union demands in London. The workforce accepted the closure almost unanimously on 3 September – a vote "to end the only way of life they knew. It was very hard. Perhaps that is why it was such a dignified, human event." Others experienced "a sense of relief that nine months of rumour, uncertainty, and frequent changes in plans could now be brought to an end. The anxiety had seemed like a chinese water torture and they longed for it to end." So the works closed on 14 September 1980. Yet trying to implement closure in only two weeks resulted in "one appalling turmoil of uncertainty and anxiety". The problem was that some people were needed to stay on after closure to accomplish run-down procedures. Normal communications broke down as arguments broke out over redundancy terms in relation to those who would stay on for a short while. Dismissal notices for those who would leave at closure were finally issued only the day before closure.

> Lists were prepared of greater or less willing volunteers; notices were issued; most people were able to leave. They left with a sense of relief mixed with pain. In losing their employment people suffered many losses, not all of which were appreciated until later. Many left with a sense of distress at the abrupt and unceremonious ending of near on a lifetime of work with one organization. These were strange days combining an atmosphere a bit like Christmas Eve together with a great enormous sadness. Photographers and samplers abounded . . . On the Friday evening a piper played a lament all around the works. On the Saturday the last coke oven was pushed . . . three thousand people went out of the gates for the last time.

Why should this story be told? Today the steelworks is grassed over; the land reclaimed; new industry has sprung up. Unemployment is still high, but for many civil servants Consett is a success story. Indeed one civil servant said that the West German civil service approached the Department of Trade and Industry in the North-East to learn how the transition was made. Consett is now a cleaner, greener place than it ever was. So why should one hark back to nine years ago?

There are many reasons why this story should be told: indeed, John Eyles's narrative is much longer than this, and much of the emotional poignancy is lost in the abbreviation of it. The story should be remembered because the North-East has endured a litany of closures since 1945. Before that there were poverty and depression: works were shut but re-opened eventually, though some inevitably closed for good. However, the way of life did not end. After 1945 in coal, in shipbuilding and in steel the North-East endured wave after wave of closures. There were good times in between, much modest prosperity and new housing, there were new factories and old jobs. Yet again and again the closures returned, like the Vikings, sweeping in from the sea a thousand years earlier, who also ended a way of life.

Today in 1989, the closures have almost ended. There is no more steel in Spennymoor or Consett; only a few pits left on the coast, employing less than ten thousand men (in 1957 coal employed over one hundred thousand in Co. Durham); no shipbuilding on the Tees or the Wear, and only a few thousand shipbuilders on the Tyne, who grow fewer each year. One very modern steelworks survives on Teesside, and employs a third of the workforce compared with fifteen years ago, yet produces as much steel.

So the way of life has now changed. No longer is it a hard, industrial area, with pride in the coal mines, steel mills and shipyards which once so dominated the horizon. Today, and irrevocably, the region has its future in car plants, light industry, tourism and the service industry. Such an experience for an entire region raises the most acute issues for Christian mission. Few areas can have changed so drastically in a couple of decades. (Indeed, the open-air museum at Beamish which recreates the way of life in the region when coal, steel and shipbuilding were at their height in the 1920s has become a North-East shrine, where children can learn how once their ancestors lived, and union rallies are held there amidst the relics of the past.) As one recent study, aptly called *Post-Industrial Tyneside*,[2] put it:

> Change now really is all pervasive and fundamental ... The old and the familiar is being swept away. Tyneside's traditional industries are nearly gone, council housing is being marginalized and privatised. Education is undergoing major changes, as is the health service, through privatisation. Change is equally prevalent in other aspects of life such as the rise in violent crime; the decline of organised religion; the rising rate of divorce.

Where is Christian mission in all of this? The story of Consett is not unique. Indeed, John Eyles wrote another piece about the drastically sudden closure of the Caterpillar plant at Birtley with the title "Another Year, Another Closure 1983–4". A similar story is told in a report by the coal industry chaplain in the North-East, Stephen Kendal, on the miners' strike of 1984–5. The strike was preceded by many closures, and followed by another round of redundancies, and the end of many pits. If, now, this seems like the end of a particular culture, the trauma of that time should not be forgotten.

The issues for Christian mission are about how economic and social life shape who we are and how we live as individuals and as a community. Could the pain of the Consett closure have been handled any differently, let alone the violence and bitterness of the miners' strike? What place had the Church in all these events? What should be said to the inevitable casualties of this process, who are the long-term unemployed and the young people ill-trained for a society which offers well-paid jobs to the highly skilled, and very little indeed to the unskilled? What, too, should be said about the new entrepreneurs, who realize that the old order has now gone far more irrevocably than during the closures and Depression of the 1930s? Can there be a Christian welcome for those who create wealth by means of shopping centres, light industry and "heritage" tourism?

The last paragraph puts these issues in the form of questions, because the new era which is slowly emerging has sharply divided the churches. The churches could agree that unemployment was "undesirable" and that unemployment schemes were to be welcomed, though some questioned how much the Church compromised itself in being involved with government schemes. However, there was no agreement as to whether closures should be opposed by the churches, and John Eyles was actually dismissed as chaplain to Caterpillar by the management during this closure. There is even less consensus as to whether the new, and fragile, prosperity should mean that the economic strategies of modern tycoons are to be welcomed by the churches.

If these are problematic questions, there is another debate which is interwoven with them in an inextricable way. How does the involvement of the churches as official bodies, with official representatives through industrial chaplains or church leaders, relate to the mission of the Church? How too do individual Christians, or half-believers in the contemporary and ambiguously secular world, see their faith in God and their hopes for a better society as in any way part of their daily life at work? Do the churches have any justification for their involvement in industrial and economic life? Can mission include a proper concern for the social, the economic and the industrial life of contemporary society?

Thus Industrial Mission becomes more than an idea, or even than a fairly large number of full or part-time chaplains. It is where the events told in stories of suffering and hope touch the life of the Church. It is where the difficult and controversial debates about economic life become part of Christian living. It is where the daily working-out of the market of its creation of wealth is seen as something of great concern to the purposes of God. The free market is seen by some as a force to be strenuously opposed, while by others it is welcomed. But Industrial Mission is always to be understood in the context of stories like Consett. Other stories could be more hopeful, about the creation of new communities. Nevertheless it is the countless number of stories, hopeful and despairing, told by Industrial Chaplains which locate the movement. Why then is it there? Is it time to look back nearly fifty years, to the foundation of Industrial Mission in Sheffield between 1941 and 1944.

The Changes in Industrial Mission

The recent report *IM – An Appraisal* discusses the nature of mission in industrial mission.[3] What is the "M" in "IM", it asks? The report quotes Adrian Hastings, who wrote about Leslie Hunter, Bishop of Sheffield. Hunter is seen by Hastings as a crucial leader in the new interpretation of mission. Hunter was appalled at the gulf between the Church and most of society; he noticed especially the chasm between the Church and the working classes. He envisaged a partnership between clergy and lay people, so that there could be a "new evangelism" and a new order, in both Church and society. His diocesan letter of November 1941 called for a new beginning. By 1944 he had appointed E. R. Wickham as the leader of the Sheffield "Industrial Mission". Hastings comments that at the time it was certainly not

> a major piece of Anglican policy-making. In retrospect it would nevertheless be recognised as the start of something important in the creation of a "missionary structure" for the Church's presence in a modern urban-industrial community.

The recent collection of essays about Leslie Hunter makes the same point.[4] Leslie Hunter rejected the report *Towards the Conversion of England*, written in 1946. This report spelt out a strategy for evangelism. Hunter believed that the alienation of the working class was profound. Therefore a new strategy would be needed in relating to those on the factory floor, far removed from any contact with the Church. However, the movement which Hunter and Wickham began grew far beyond the early beginnings in Sheffield, although they were both to be associated with it over many years.

Mostyn Davies traces the evolution of Industrial Mission since it began.[5] The first-generation work in the Victorian era was pastoral and evangelistic. This approach is still found in the work of the Missions to Seamen. The second generation, discussed above, put chaplains on to the factory floor. This resulted in much discussion of the ethics of industrial relations, which was a controversial area. IM (Industrial Mission) work became professional, since it required great expertise to work in this area. It was a turning-point, for it was an end to a view of IM as an extension of the parish system. Chaplains were criticized by those who disliked their ecumenical, world-affirming theology and their role. Equally the political concerns of many chaplains were a form of ethical socialism. In turn chaplains criticized the old religious language and patterns of thought, claiming they were unintelligible to most urban people. Increasingly IM began to be separate from mainstream church life. At the same time IM came to regard parochial life as irrelevant, and charted its decreasing influence in terms of churchgoing. Edward Wickham's book *Church and People in an Industrial City*, published in 1957, provided the intellectual justification. It was a well-argued book, although it entirely predated the arguments of David Martin, Robin Gill and others on how religious this country actually was. All its chapters made a correlation between membership figures (or rites of passage numbers in baptisms, weddings and funerals) and what is called influence; prophecy; and dialogue. Wickham called for more study of the "effect of modern society upon the mind and spirits of men and on . . . the working-class culture pattern".[6] These "all-pervasive and determining factors that can enslave men or liberate them" Wickham called "Principalities and powers". Yet there is no analysis at all in the book of the non-churchgoing religiosity so acutely analysed by David Martin, and the book's sections on "scepticism", the scientific spirit and the effects of the First

World War paint with too broad a brush.

Nevertheless the importance of the book was in demonstrating that the churches were far weaker than they appeared to be. Wickham fought passionately for a lay movement, where people of good will would discuss the issues of the day. "If this concept is not entirely illusory, ten years of concentrated work based upon common policy could establish the Church in an industrial society in an entirely new way."[7] Wickham was to be disappointed: IM became a movement predominantly run by clergy. However, Wickham was also unwilling to let the official Church get too close to the movement which sprang up in the 1950s. Other chaplains had different styles: there was no one agreed strategy.[8]

In the late 1970s the picture changed dramatically. Until then there had been a sharp disagreement on the manner in which the Church should relate to industry, but it was always assumed that industrial life, while changing all the time, would remain. Now the entire picture changed. As Chris Beals, then an industrial chaplain in Hartlepool and later Secretary to the Industrial Committee of the Church of England, wrote in 1984:

> With regard to the wider Church, IM across the country is finding that, with the advent of mass unemployment, many of the skills and contacts developed over the years by chaplains and people involved with IM are first what the local congregations, deaneries and councils of churches want. We could easily spend all our time, very usefully on the issue of unemployment, helping others to respond, etc. But who then would do the much more difficult job of trying to relate the Gospel to the world of industry, technology and work?[9]

For a while IM seemed to find all its new initiatives in working with the unemployed. While much traditional factory visiting went on, a whole range of training programmes began. Clearly this work helped the wider Church to recognize the value of IM, although the old tensions remained underneath. However, eventually unemployment began to fall nationally, although it remains high in Northern towns. The government turned to private contractors who would place the long-term unemployed with employers. The number of young people declined also in the labour market. Therefore, the 1980s end with a challenge to IM. How does it see its role in the future, where unemployment in the South and Midlands at least is no longer a major issue?

Industrial Mission and Mission

The 1988 review of Industrial Mission, entitled *IM – An Appraisal*, was not just one more Church report. It was the first review of IM's work since the pioneering days of 1944–59, which culminated in the last report, now thirty years old, *The Task of the Church in Relation to Industry* (1959). This report was written by Edward Wickham and introduced to the Church Assembly by Leslie Hunter. Thus the movement in its first decade and a half was dominated by a few individuals. While there were many other chaplains, nearly all the pioneers had begun in Sheffield under these two men.

Thirty years on, there are new questions to be considered. What is the future for IM in the next decade? Clearly that question will be decided by the churches, by IM teams, by those whose experience goes back now many decades. All this chapter can do is to offer a few theological reflections on the two narratives set out above, the closure at Consett and the development of IM from 1944 to 1988. A number of chaplains and theologians have joined in this debate in recent years.[10] At issue is the nature of mission, given that the old working-class culture has gone. This culture once pervaded industrial life, and led a workers' committee of a large Sheffield steel mill in 1941 to reject a visit by Bishop Hunter since there was no past evidence that the Church had shown any interest in helping the working class.[11]

Today such a culture is increasingly a memory. As Mostyn Davies writes,

> Where yesterday's economic and political forces created a collectivised, working-class, shop-floor culture and trade-union solidarity, now they create a new world of offices, shops and warehouses, an aspiring middle-class culture and a spirit of property-owning individualism ... at least, for the "haves". The "have-nots" form a twenty per cent underclass of dependent, pressurized people whose economic realities (and so much of their health and happiness) are determined for them by DHSS rules, Family Credit, Income Support, Restart interviews, housing problems, debt and low-paid work. The priority task for IM is to help the Church address the ethical and spiritual issues raised by these new economic realities and the dominant New Right philosophy which gives use to them.[12]

Davies would therefore abandon the earlier hope of a lay movement. He would hope IM would analyse the local economy with universities or council planning departments, discern priorities and then set up activities such as job-creation or training projects. Elsewhere factory visiting may continue. The issue will be whether "the powerless [can] get a grip on events and obtain some purchase on their own destinies". A review of these activities would watch for signs of collusion, dependency and the serving of local vested interests.

The theology of mission which underlies this is different from the one developed in the 1950s to 1960s. The previous one was "about liberating working men from drudgery and expanding their human potential within a more democratic and caring industrial order". The new theology advocated is close to liberation theology, working with an underclass manipulated by economic forces. "The salvation element in this type of theology is not personalized." Instead the concern is to echo the Old Testament's demand for justice in the land. "Redemption" is appropriate language for what redeems the social disorder of a nation. Evangelism is rejected in this theory:

> IM has not been evangelistic in Britain. This reflects IM's early experience of the great alienation and bitterness felt by working people as the result of their exposure to crude, judgemental revivalism. Evangelistic chaplains would have been instantly rejected from the place of work and would still be. In contrast with this alienation, IM has found a positive approach to the Church's attempt at pursuing and advocating social justice and improvement to the quality of life.[13]

Mission therefore is related to evangelism in this model, but it is a different vocation. Personal salvation and the pursuit of holiness are not the main aims. The mission would potentially be drawn into a mass of church-based activity. Further, lay Christians are spread out in industrial life. They are constrained by their employers. Therefore they cannot be effective agents for change as a group. Individuals may however have great impact. Davies prefers to build up a group working with the disadvantaged, rather than work with individuals. This group will be separate from those who are committed to the Church, but in sympathy with its values. Furthermore, Christian lay people will be discovered "on the job", but only as part of the strategy to work with the poor and powerless.

Davies offers one of the most coherent theories of mission for IM, though its relationship with the local church is hardly stressed at all. A similar vision is described by Margaret Kane, who was Theological Consultant in North-East England from 1969 to 1981, and before that a member of Sheffield Industrial Mission. Again the influence of Bishop Leslie Hunter was strong in her earlier career. She writes of the influence on her own ministry in the 1950s, of the French sociologists who studied the gulf between the Church and the working class. As a result of this influence she responded to an invitation by Bishop Hunter, and worked for seven years in a mining parish in his diocese, and then for seven years visiting factories in Sheffield. She describes the fatalism of the urban working class, and the irrelevance of belief in God to their salvation.

> If Christian faith is to be presented as a point of view about life and as a way of life for people in these circumstances, and with this background of misunderstanding and unbelief, theological insights and skills of a high order are required.[14]

In her latest book, *What Kind of God?*, which is the last of a trilogy published from 1975 to 1986,[15] she looks back on her ministry so "that the new vision of God which is required in an urban society can be spelt out more clearly". IM for her from 1959 to 1966 was primarily evangelistic, for she wanted to help people outside the influence of the Church "to come to a living faith".[16] She spent three years in Hong Kong from 1966 to 1969, beginning IM there. On her return to England, she found that the evangelism she had espoused, with its opposition to social injustice and criticism of the inwardness of the Church, was no longer accepted. "Evangelism was now seen not as related to but as opposed to prophecy." Why, she asked herself, was this so? In part it was because there was more cynicism about the possibility of creating a better world than in the period after 1945. The Church itself was far weaker. Above all the Church and IM had developed different theologies: the vision of IM is of a response to the Kingdom, where the Church is to be a sign revealing the nature of the Kingdom. The parochial church system was seen as only preaching a gospel of individual salvation. For Margaret Kane the Trinitarian understanding of God means that Jesus Christ reveals the nature of God's activity with humanity. The Church for her is a community which witnesses to Jesus, but seeks the sign of the Kingdom in the world, and "getting involved in the misery of the world".

> The church is not simply a human instition but a ... fellowship within which we already experience the joy of table fellowship with Christ and his Saints. The glory of God which will be revealed in all its fulness at the end, already penetrates the world and human life.[17]

IM is weakest for Margaret Kane when it tries to go beyond analysis. It is good at working alongside people in industry and unemployment, denying the pervasive fatalism by holding out the possibility of change. Prophecy discerns the key issues in the light of God's judgement, looking at whatever devalues the worth of people in large organizations, whether they are children in schools, clients in social services or workers in industry. Evangelism asks about the place of the individual in all this, and how he or she will look for change in the light of God's purposes. Too much evangelism, in Margaret Kane's analysis, is weighed down with a domesticated, churchy sense of God in our culture. Equally she rejects many parish churches as being committed to individual salvation. Like Davies, she now feels that IM has spent too much time relating to the Church, in many different ways. Clergy were taken round industry, ordinands worked with IM teams, industrial chaplains worked with congregational groups or assisted on Sundays. She wishes IM to create new and provisional forms of the Church dispersed in the world. These would be groups of Christians and non-Christians, who would seek to strive for justice, reflect on their experiences in industry and society and support each other. Worship would be a matter for each group, while Christians would also continue to worship in their own churches.[18]

Margaret Kane, like Mostyn Davies, draws heavily on liberation theology. On salvation, she quotes Bonino: "Jesus Christ does not come to superimpose a different, transcendent, or celestial reality on top of the realm of nature and history but to reopen for man the will and power to fulfil his historical vocation ... to man."[19] Unlike recent liberation theologians, however, she feels British theology needs to spend less time developing a spirituality than continuing the quest for political involvement. Above all she stresses the way of doing theology for everyone, reflecting on experience, analysing it systematically, seeing the experiences in various expressions of the Christian faith, and acting upon these.[20] She returns to the way in which IM works with people deeply suspicious of church life, who make contact with industrial chaplains to discuss practical issues of social and industrial life, such as industrial relations, unemployment, etc. It was these people whom she sought to interest in theology. Yet her experience was bleak: much of her book is about small-scale successes and achievements, while on the wider church front she writes: "it was over the issue of the contribution of lay people to theology that I clashed most often and most fundamentally with those who controlled church policies in the North-East."[21]

The answer given by Davies and Kane to the question of mission places great emphasis on alleviating powerlessness, and valuing the experience of ordinary people. "If God is to be found anywhere he must be found in and through 'ordinary' things and 'ordinary' people. Our search for God must be, not primarily by considering 'religious matters', but by digging deeply into human experience."[22] Kane points to a shared identity between matters of basic, human concern and a Christianity which requires discipleship of Jesus Christ. She advocates both traditional churches and "intermediate groups" of people with a common concern, which may be that of action, reflection, endurance or spiritual searching. Some of these groups will have no affiliation with local congregations while others will. She believes the most important task is to offer resources to enable people to reflect on their experience and to find God for themselves. IM's main contribution, then, would be to create provisional expressions of the Church as dispersed in the world.[23] Davies looks for social justice, again drawing on liberation theology and on the Old Testament analysis of corporate wrongdoing. He too no longer wishes to place much emphasis on relating to the Church, though he rejoices in Christians who do join him in the work of being alongside the poor and dispossessed. There is less emphasis in his work on doing theology with ordinary people in small groups.

These two writers have shaped the consciousness of IM powerfully, both by their work in it (Mostyn Davies began in 1969, Margaret Kane in 1959) and by their writings (Mostyn Davies mainly by articles, Margaret Kane by her three books.)[24] The 1988 report on IM was deeply aware of the tensions between the local church and IMs. It mentioned Margaret Kane's belief that there would inevitably be tension between the Church gathered for worship in its traditional form, and the Church dispersed in the world, affirming the life of the unemployed and employed, the poor and disadvantaged and those at the creative centre of our culture. Such tension could allow questions, discovery and growth, but also conflict.[25] There is therefore a profound issue about the nature of mission. If the Church is in dialogue with the world, can IM be part of the Church? Kane's answer is "yes", but only if you accept conflict and tension. In the previous chapter, certain criticisms of mission by Lindbeck and Roberts were spelt out. At the same time a different, although perhaps complementary rather than contradictory, vision of the Church given by Vanstone and Hauerwas was described. Kane and Davies have an understanding of mission in which tension is endemic between different parts of the Church.

Yet the tension in the 1988 report on IM was not simply about its relationship to the Church. As mentioned earlier in this chapter, there is also controversy about the attitude which should be taken to the creation of wealth, and political involvement. There is still the question of how industrial chaplains (whether lay or ordained, employed by the Church full-time or part-time) relate to lay Christians in industry. Thus the 1990s will re-open the debate of the 1950s and 1960s, which was partially terminated by the need to respond to the unemployment crisis nationally of the late 1970s to 1980s (locally of course there is still high unemployment).

Has the movement launched by Hunter, and developed with great forcefulness by Wickham in the 1950s in Sheffield, now come to mean an almost institutionalized tension in the mission of the Church? Can it say anything positive about evangelism and the local congregation? The local church has changed since 1944. In some places, though not by any means in all, there is an understanding of social division, social responsibility and involvement in industrial life. "Salvation" would include notions of social justice for some Evangelicals today. Can the local church accept that these aspects of mission are best performed by specialist chaplains? Or is it the future one of continuous mistrust, repeating on the issue of the Church's attitude to the world the controversies, which have racked the churches since the Reformation, over predestination, salvation and the role of the Church in the world's relationship to God? If so, the movement which Hunter began with realism but also with optimism will turn out to have been a divisive force inside the Church, as well as a movement which achieved much in terms of social justice. Theologically two different accounts of mission are given here. One describes how the local church responds to the love of God. The other sees the Church as a champion of the poor and powerless. Yet justice and the love of God should not be set apart. There needs to be no opposition between them, but in practice, and often in theory, they symbolize vastly different viewpoints. For many industrial chaplains, the debate is irrelevant. All that matters is how the commitment to the poor is made, and whether there is any place left for factory visiting. For others the dispute outlined above is still one worth discussing, and some industrial chaplains do play an active role in parishes, although they may well experience the hostility of other, more evangelical churches. Such chaplains tend to resolve the tension pragmatically and get on with "the real issue", such as the job-training scheme or factory visiting which is close at hand.

How did the report itself resolve these tensions? In part the answer was again that it did so pragmatically. But there was also an attempt to wrestle theologically with questions of mission. The report describes one volatile meeting of chaplains across a region. There was a whole variety of responses: the Church is here; we are the Church; IM looked down on parishes; when people learnt he was leaving to go into IM, they regarded him as a heretic; if IM isn't understood . . . the Church does not want to hear. The respondent commented "One of the key areas for the working party [writing the report] is surely how IM can be part of the whole mission of the Church, and it seems to me that this is blocked by some of the perceptions I've noted here."[26] The report subsequently affirmed "the need to discern the moment when speaking of faith may lead to greater understanding", and rejected the view that the Church was "so far to blame for the alienation of working people from its life that nothing overt may be said about the Christian faith because it will alienate people."[27] Equally it criticized any church which did not look for the social implications of the Gospel and for the discovery of Jesus in the workplace.

But what sort of church should this be theologically, and what sort of mission? The report mentioned the theology of Kane and Davies, although lack of space prevented any systematic analysis of their views. Therefore the report looked at ways of involving lay people in IM. Groups could meet at work or go away for a weekend. They could join a project for social justice. They could meet with other people in the country to discuss certain issues. It noted the Roman Catholic view that it was entirely the role of the laity to live out their faith in industry, while the role of priests is to help them make connections with their faith outside the workplace. The chapter on the Church ended up by looking at the task of the chaplain in industry; does he or she seek to establish a gathered congregation in industry, or encourage lay people to form links with IM; or is he or she sent out as a lone missionary ahead of the Church, with the possibility of losing touch with the Church altogether in the demanding struggle to find God in the secular industrial world? (He or she may lose faith altogether as well, at least in any traditional sense.)[28] What was needed, however, in the report was to talk more of the local church's relationship to IM. Equally the chapter on mission ended up by commending IM for refusing to manipulate its audience and for its willingness to serve wherever it discerned a need. The report discussed the language which the Church must use in worldly places. This is deeply important. Yet what of the dichotomy in the nature of mission raised by Margaret Kane and Mostyn Davies? A report can only indicate where the tensions lie. Thus it ended by arguing that mission must include a response to industrial and economic forces, for they affect everyone and it is God's world. Consequently "it is the responsibility of the whole Church to ensure that its missionary policies in the industrial and economic field are properly integrated with all other aspects of mission and ministry".[29] The report drew the attention of the whole Church to the contribution of IM to the Church's mission, at a critical time for IM. But the debate on the theological tension between the mission of the local church and a mission to do with industry still remains to be resolved.

The relationship of these two aspects of mission focuses attention on the meaningfulness of talk of God today. Christian belief is a form of action, embodying intentions and values. Reflecting on these actions has theoretical implications, which result in theology. It is not that there is a correct theory about God, which some apply to a style of life called mission to the individual, and others to mission to society. Instead I would wish to disagree with Margaret Kane's belief that wrong models of God lead to incorrect patterns of ministry. I believe that there are many ways of living the Christian life, and that each of them can be called a story about what God did in Jesus Christ. The crucial question is to discern when telling the story in different ways becomes telling a different story altogether. Christians tell the story of Jesus Christ. In telling that story they will refer to the life of the Church, for that is part of the story. There are many ways to tell the story, depending on one's theological tradition, culture, social background, etc. We begin in the Church with acts which are a sharing of Christ's love and hope for the people around Him, and His obedience to the Father. We begin with action: "that a thing is true is no reason that it should be said but that it should be done".[30] Our action is in a living-out of the Gospel, as handed on to us in a living tradition. The Gospel is not simply the biblical text, nor the written tradition, but the Good News about God and this world, as embodied in a previous generation's set of actions . . . and so back to the life of Jesus, and before that the people of Israel. This faith is recorded in the Biblical text and the traditional documents of the Church. In the life of Jesus God was present irrevocably, so that Jesus was later seen as the revelation of God for us: the incarnation of the eternal in time. We live out our lives in history, and as we do so, we open ourselves to a greater or lesser degree to this Gospel, or text. If the ordinary course of our lives as individuals leads us to explore what this Gospel means, we join a community. Corporately we live out this Gospel, and like actors with a script we begin to perform the text. But there is no one way to perform a play which is the definitive performance. Different actors will play the text differently. Yet they all reveal different parts of the story: they are telling the story differently. At this point the question arises as to whether it is possible to perform a text in such a different way that it becomes a different story, not a new performance which tells the same story differently.

So assessing such things is very difficult, though we are not excused the effort. The implication for the relationship of local church to IM is that the one needs the other for the living-out of the Gospel in action. Without the exposure to worship, the tradition of the Church and communal existence, a performance of the text or Gospel by industrial chaplains in the secular world may have much to do with justice but will begin to find talk of God increasingly difficult. This has repeatedly been the case with

IM. (This is not the place for a review of the "God who acts" school of Biblical theology used by industrial chaplains in the 1950s, but it is safe to say that it was demolished as decisively as an obsolete factory building by theologians such as Lindbeck, Kelsey and Frei in the 1970s. Although this demolition intellectually was not picked up by IM, it left their talk of God acting in historical change close to a form of mythological piety.) Without the exposure to the reality of social change and deprivation, more traditional churches will find their language vacuous and disengaged, and this can be hard to accept.

My vision of IM is that it is the tool of the whole Church for wrestling with questions of profound human creativity and alienation in the world, as particularly focused in industry. The language of creativity is given meaning by the concrete reality of technological change, social co-operation and new forms of wealth creation. Creativity can be shown in new ways of overcoming poverty and unemployment, as in Davies's work in job-creation or the "Respond" Project on Teesside with which Margaret Kane has been associated. But IM always needs to be related closely to the churches. This is not a pragmatic point, but a theological one. Canon Bill Hall set up through the Impasse programme (with a team whom he drew together) many centres where people could explore their creativity in woodwork, metalwork and many other hobbies. These were used by the unemployed, but he refused to see them as centres for the unemployed. Instead they were places where creativity could be expressed outside of paid employment. Creativity can also be found in the creation of wealth, as Canon John Atherton has recently argued in his recent book, *Faith in the Nation*.[31] Talk of creativity must be related to a theology of change and blessing, where the future of a person or object is affirmed in the way appropriate to it. It is in wrestling with these issues that the local church is challenged to ask what its belief in the presence of God in material life actually involves. Relating the ever more complex transformation of our material and social life by human beings to the vision of God's care and future blessing in Scripture puts faith to the utmost test.

The Church performs the text at the heart of its life. The text is the Gospel. The performance is the living out of the Gospel in worship, evangelism, mission and pastoral care. Without this enactment the Church becomes a purely social institution. The world is the audience, although the dichotomy of Church/world is not absolute (as argued in Chapter 2). The world is a partner in this exploration,[32] even allowing for the danger of the Church becoming too much immersed in the world so that the Christian faith becomes hard to identify. This is not faint-heartedness: it is to point to the very real difficulties of a "secular theology" in Britain in the 1980s. The difficulty lies in the way religious language has meaning only when embodied in the action of those who corporately believe in God. During the forty years since Industrial Mission began, there has been a growing difficulty of using religious talk in the secular world. Talk of social justice, powerlessness and helping the poor is entirely right when a chaplain raises issues in the workplace, but lying behind these discussions will be the question of the authority of the chaplain – and ultimately the question of the reality of God. "The stage on which we enact our performance is that wider human history in which the Church exists as the 'sacrament' or dramatic enactment of history's ultimate meaning and hope."[33] But is there any hope, any hope at all?

The debate on the report on Industrial Mission in the Church of England's General Synod in July 1989 reiterated these points. The Church needs Industrial Mission so that it can speak to people at work, and understand their world. It can assist people in turmoil, as in Consett, work with them in poverty and discern the ethical dilemmas of those with wealth and power. It should help the Church to prophesy, to care and to be present at the heart of the economic order, working with those with wealth and those at the margins, showing Christians how to connect their faith and their daily life. Thus it asks the question of the local church: what does your faith mean in the secular, urban, industrial life of today? This was the issue raised above all by Archbishop John Habgood. That question is raised in countless personal experiences, but Industrial Mission provides one structured way of having a dialogue in the modern world. Only out of this dialogue can mission in the modern world be one which is serious about its own faith and the integrity of the world. The Synod debate praised Industrial Mission for its concern for the poor. The changing economic life of Britain will mean changes in Industrial Mission, and a need to support the poor and to assist those in positions of responsibility. Always, as the Synod debate noted, there will be a need to help Christians relate their faith to their daily life and work.

CHAPTER 6

Pastoral Care and Unity

a compassion that was timeless and without mercy.

> William Golding, *Pincher Martin*

You can't conceive, my child, nor can I or anyone the . . . appalling . . . strangeness of the mercy of God.

> Graham Greene, *Brighton Rock*

> We do not like to look out of the same window,
>   and see quite a different landscape,
> We do not like to climb a stair, and find
>   that it takes us down.
> We do not like to walk out of a door, and
>   find ourselves back in the same room.
> We do not like the maze in the garden, because
>   it too closely resembles the maze in the brain.
>
> So the knot be unknotted,
> The crossed be uncrossed,
> The crooked be made straight,
> And the curse be ended
> By intercession
> By pilgrimage
> By those who depart
> In several directions
> For their own redemption
> And that of the departed –
>   May they rest in peace.
>
> T. S. Eliot, *The Family Reunion*

Introduction

In 1986, during a round of pit closures, including the announcement of the closure of Horden Colliery in Co. Durham, the Consultancy published a study of the effects of pit closures from the point of view of local people, the clergy in the area, the District Council and the management of British Coal.[1] It was a response to a survey of the social and economic costs of closure by the Geography Department of the University of Durham, undertaken at the invitation of the District Council.[2]

One of the comments which was made most strongly in the Consultancy report came from a mother in the area. She spoke for many others:

> As parents we watch our children grow up. Teaching them right from wrong, worrying about their education, and where they will eventually take their place in modern society. Our son is now 18½ years of age, with no hopes of being employed. He was an average pupil at school, and was employed on a Youth Training Scheme for a year taking motor vehicle mechanics. Having gained his first part City and Guilds he was eager to learn and very happy with life. Since then, however, apart from a few months working as a labourer he has been unemployed. Is he now to face a life of unemployment? Our son has an added disadvantage because he suffers from a slight skin disorder, whereupon he usually fails a medical examination. We hear him say "What chance do I stand of ever working?" It makes one feel very bitter and guilty, bringing children into a world of disappointment and heartbreak. There is no one to put a word in for him or to help him. He is getting depressed. He is just one of the many condemned to a life on the dole.

This was echoed by another lady who said; "Over the years Church leaders have tended to command a lot of respect in communities such as ours, faced with such an uncertain future. Any support we get from the Church will help to relieve our despair." Male unemployment in this area has been at 15–20% for many years: while three years after this report it has fallen back, it was still the case in 1988 that the percentage of unemployed benefit claimants out of work for more than three years in the Northern Region was stable at 23% during 1987–8, well above the national average. It is also the case that more than 40% had been out of work for more than one year; that it was one of the worst areas in terms of the chances of leaving unemployment, and the likelihood of becoming unemployed remains higher in the Northern Region than in Great Britain.[3] All these figures would certainly be true of Easington District. There is growing prosperity in the North-East, and some sense of hope, but in some areas there is still a feeling of acute hopelessness. More pits will almost certainly close in the next few years, leaving the area with high long-term unemployment. It is not simply in inner-city areas, but in other local districts untouched by the "enterprise culture", that unemployment remains high. Even where new jobs do come, and the ethic of self-employment spreads, there is so much past unemployment that the future must remain very bleak.

There are several implications for pastoral care and mission in this survey. First, there is the fact that personal suffering is the result of social changes. The first chapter of this book showed that the pastoral needs of men and women can be either very individual, expressed in problems such as divorce or an inability to form relationships, or on the other hand deeply determined by the social disintegration around them. Secondly, there is the question of who ministers to people in need. One of the great strengths of recent writing about mission is the emphasis on mission and pastoral care being a responsibility for the whole congregation, working with the community outside the church. (Indeed, such a division will often be hard to maintain in many communities.) This stress is there in both Robin Greenwood's book and Laurie Green's. Thirdly, there is the fact that it was a group of women who most powerfully spelt out the implications for personal well-being in the prospect of future closures of mines and growing long-term unemployment. There can no longer be any generalized perspective on pastoral care, or mission. It is increasingly the case that women are showing that older assumptions have to be rethought. Finally, there is the fact that pastoral care is something on which a united Christian presence is essential. The contributors to the Consultancy study on Easington were an Anglican parish priest and an Anglican industrial chaplain (who worked ecumenically), a Methodist minister and a Roman Catholic youth chaplain, who all lived in the area. The forewords to the report were written by the Anglican Bishop of Durham, David Jenkins; the Methodist Chairman of the Darlington District, Geoffrey Kemp; and the Roman Catholic Bishop of Hexham and Newcastle, Hugh Lindsey, with the leader of the District Council, John Cummings (a Roman Catholic, and now MP for the area). Mission and ecumenism are interrelated, for ecumenism is for the sake of mission, yet any strategy of mission which is not ecumenical is not merely weaker in a pragmatic sense, but also loses the sense of Christian community, which has been called Koinonia.

Therefore this chapter will explore the relationship between mission, pastoral care and work in the community; it will look at the different perspective offered by feminist writers, and the stress on lay ministry; and it will seek to find the ecumenical context of mission. All this however must be always related to a theology of the local church responding to the love of God in all its richness, and to the encounter with industrial and technological change in Industrial Mission. These are not different strategies for mission, but aspects of one whole. Without the local church, there can be no encounter with the immediate community; without the challenge put by Industrial Mission the encounter of church and community can become unrelated to profound social and economic change, and the church becomes only an instance of a past social order; without pastoral care churches will be asked "what is the point of it all?" Phil Brown's challenge remains. We begin with the community setting of social change.

Deprivation in the Community

As social research has progressed in Britain, certain ways of measuring material deprivation, or poverty, have evolved. Sociologists investigate communities with unemployment (for men in Townsend's survey this was between the ages of sixteen and sixty-four, for women between the ages of sixteen and fifty-nine); they measure the extent of car ownership, for where public transport is bad, car ownership is often an indication of the level of disposable income; they examine the level of home ownership, again as a way of trying to see how affluent an area is; and finally they look at the extent of overcrowding, with more than one person per room. All these are ambiguous indices of affluence or poverty, but they do serve to indicate what level of prosperity or poverty there is in an area. Professor Peter Townsend of Bristol University published a report in 1986 drawing on this work. He related ill-health to the community's level of poverty. Each of the 678 wards in the Northern Regional Health Authority was analyzed in terms of a formula derived from the four marks of deprivation listed above. Each of the 678 wards is then grouped into five equal-sized groupings (called quantiles) measuring the degree of deprivation. Then Townsend analyzed three criteria for ill-health, and ranked the 678 wards in quantiles of ill-health. The three criteria were "High levels of premature mortality", where Townsend found ten per cent of wards with adult premature mortality as bad as the mortality rate of Britain in 1950[4]; permanent sickness, which is of course based on self-reporting but where the Northern Region fared very badly compared with England and Wales as a whole[5]; and low birth weight, measured as under 6lb or 2800 grammes.[6]

What impressed Townsend and his team was that the correlation between deprivation and ill health was always there. If you lived in a ward in the bottom fifth on ill health, so too it would be one of the worst fifth in material terms. Conversely the healthiest areas are – always – those with most cars, home ownership; least overcrowding and least unemployment. Simply by measuring the degree of car and house ownership, and knowing the level of unemployment and overcrowding, you can tell what percentage of babies will be born underweight. This will not be exact, but you can predict in which quintile the ward will be.

Not surprisingly, people find this very hard to take. I remember vividly an evening meeting where I talked about this report in one of the villages (wards) with the worst health problems. Again and again people in the church meeting rejected these arguments. Ill health is a personal thing, they argued: people have small babies for family reasons. Equally if people die early, that is because there were many chronically sick people in the village. Yet half of Easington District's population of 97,000 lives in the worst quintile, and a third lives in the worst tenth, in terms of both deprivation and ill health.

Professor Townsend is quite clear that the attempt to close villages and move people away as the pits closed from 1954 to 1969 was a failure. He writes "Ill health goes hand-in-hand with such social and economic marginality".[7] People remained in the villages, but the reversal of the policy in 1970 was too late. Unemployment rose across County Durham as a whole. The report describes vividly the village of Wheatley Hill in County Durham: it "had three times as many people unemployed, more than ten times as many households without a car, more than fifteen times as many overcrowded households, and twelve times as many households not owning their homes as in the ward of comparable size with best health".[8] Taking a ward of roughly equal size population of 4,000 people, which was Hutton in Langbaurgh, Wheatley Hill had 52 deaths of persons under 65 in three years. Hutton had 11 such deaths. Wheatley Hill had 23 low weight births, Hutton had 9. These figures speak for themselves. Women especially between the ages of 16 to 59 die at a rate which in 1948 was the average for the whole of Britain, though no doubt Easington was worse in 1948. The main causes of death are cancer and respiratory and circulatory diseases. It is not just unhealthy eating and smoking, though no doubt that does not help. It is the fact of deprivation which is the primary cause.[9] Again, one of the quotes from the Consultancy report speaks for many: "My family has left Easington already and it was the best thing they ever did. We see some of the shops closing already."

There is a fierce local pride in the area. Unlike inner-city areas, it has a cohesive sense of belonging, and an extended family network. The local arts centre publishes much local poetry and writing:

> My husband is a miner
> To me he is my knight in shining armour
> He goes down a black hole
> So he can dig out coal
> And gets dust on his chest,
> He has sweat on his vest.[10]

However, this is a culture which celebrates an industry which is dying. Mining banners of sixty years ago speak of a distant past. This is not in any way to imply a lack of respect for this way of life, but it is not a community with a great deal of hope. The population falls, people move away, and people become cynical about the future. The Roman Catholic youth chaplain in the Consultancy report spoke of the problem which the Church faces. Religion is still a powerful force for articulating the cohesion of the community, but as it does so, it tends to be a force for inertia and lack of change. How can Christian hope be a hope for the future? Thus Jim O'Keefe notes the importance of exploring the needs and resources of the community, and the need for real solidarity with the area. He writes,

> Listening is simply not being present when things are said. Listening demands change in the hearer. We cannot listen from outside the situation, only from within it. Where there is a conflict there is a need for authentic conversation. Thus it is an exercise which has at its heart, the reality of bringing all, especially the weakest, into the life and experience of authentic participation.[11]

Mission in such a community must involve both community work and pastoral care. The two aspects are inseparable. Community work can include creating neighbourhood councils; local newspapers and information centres; mother and toddler groups, and other self-help groups; community action groups. The aim of all of these is to point to "good and positive relationships". Communities cannot be forced to look to the future, nor will they have the power to prevent decisions taken far away, such as the closure of pits. There are times when such victories are won, but they are very rare. All that community work can do is create a new sense of purpose and co-operation and thus to make a powerful statement about the density of that community. Insofar as the Church can help to provide some hope and fellowship, this is surely part of mission. As Paul Ballard writes,[12]

> Thirdly, however, as servant the Church is never an end in itself but always at the disposal of a greater reality that is universal in scope. Faithfulness includes waiting for the signs of the Master's presence. So the witness to the Kingdom includes recognizing that God, in his universal Lordship, creates anew at any time and any place. Whenever peace, justice, love, beauty is found, whenever people grow and catch a glimpse of greater possibilities, there the Kingdom

has broken through even if only fleetingly, like the moon behind clouds on a stormy night. And it is legitimate for Christians to be found at such points, rejoicing in all that happens.

The analysis above of Easington is not suggesting that all pastoral care should be seen in terms of community work. It simply suggests that very little of this has been done in the past (there are exceptions, such as the Church Army work on outer council estates and in inner cities), and much more needs to be done. However, all that this chapter can do is reflect theologically on what that might mean. Jim O'Keefe and Paul Ballard both show that community work can be part of mission.[13] The deep sociological reasons for the degree of illness in Easington demand a fully fledged response by the Church, as indeed it is beginning to make. (Nor should any of this imply that the churches have not been engaged in community work, in this area at least. Examples such as the parish church in Peterlee, or the involvement of the parish churches at Wheatley Hill, Easington Colliery, Wingate and others, come to mind.)

Yet what of the personal aspect of pastoral care? Stephen Sykes shows how in situations of crisis there is a reversion to the small scale and the domestic. A loss of horizons induces both apathy and purposelessness, but also an "acute awareness of scale". Glimpses of the reality of human joy can be found in the face or gesture of a child, a small house-plant or a domestic animal. Minor but intensely important experiences are related to "a deeply embraced identity – creating story or myth". And such a story is found in the experience of belief in Christ. In Timothy 1:1, "Jesus Christ is our hope", there is a radical theological metaphor.

> In this language the plurality and diversity of human desires are drastically reduced to a single point, a name, bearing a divine-human story. This is the focus of the Christian's world of meaning and the source of his inner strength and peace.[14]

The local church seems handicapped, because of its continual remembrance of the past glories, memories and myths. Yet at their best the churches can be models of self-help, "the more significant to the community the less they are dependent on outside resources".[15] They can provide natural support groups for those charged with looking after children, parents and the mentally ill:

> the care of the dependent has throughout Christian history sprung naturally from the instinct of compassion . . . In some of these instances a very far-reaching expression can be given of the embodiment of hope amounting even to incorporation into the Christian story, or, to put it another way, the holding of another person's story, on his or her behalf, as though already incorporated into the story of Jesus Christ.[16]

All this is daunting and demanding, and will tax the deepest resources. "Courage, perseverence and love may grow cold." The Christian community may seem not to be a community of faith, hope and charity but only a community of "thinly disguised self-interest and self-protection". Thus those who care will experience doubt and inner division. For many people caught up in caring for their neighbour and perhaps in touch with a Christian church, there will be no certainty or assurance about what they are doing. As Stanley Hauerwas has said, the reality of a relationship with God does not depend on a prior experience of religious certainty. Therefore it is appropriate to end this section on pastoral care as mission with a quotation from Peter Baelz which spells out with great perception the position of many of those who believe and yet find that the demands of pastoral care and commitment only lead to further uncertainty:

> Doubt is not done away. Is this undercurrent of doubt a symptom of his estrangement from God and his lack of love? Or may it also be a sign that his wholeness must wait upon the

wholeness of his neighbour, even of creation itself? Dare he even hope – for such indeed is his prayer – that his expectant but troubled half-belief, his experiment with life in love, an experiment which he finds himself unable either to give up or to complete, may itself minister grace to others who also find belief in God an inviting but disturbing enterprise? If he may so dare, then he will rejoice in his heart, praising and glorifying Him in whom he believes and does not believe.[17]

Lay Ministry

Laurie Green's book *Power to the Powerless* traces the development of a parish in Birmingham to the point where it decides to take action for itself. Central to this development is the discussion of Biblical passages, and their relationship to the present-day context in which these people lived. Therefore the model of experience – analysis – theological reflection–action, which leads into a further cycle, is all important. Particular attention is paid to the New Testament parables, and to the fact that "doing theology" is a form of discipleship which is essential for every Christian. In this activity there will be a place for the academically trained scholar, who may well be the parish priest, though in the contemporary church a lay person is likely to be better qualified than the parish priest. Whatever may be the case here, it is important that the "academic expert" does not dominate the discussion, but allows the experience of the group to be the central resource. The academic skills facilitate the process of reflecting on experience and its analysis: this theological reflection will draw on many resources of spirituality, Biblical discussion and contemporary Christian literature, as well as academic scholarship.[18]

The purpose of "doing theology" for everyone is that people will come to see that the Christian faith can illuminate their personal and social situations. Such illumination contains within itself the necessity of action, so that the possibilities for change and Christian commitment can be realized. Therefore the book ends with the congregation of the local church taking the initiative to set up a neighbourhood centre, and to try to change the powerlessness of those who lived literally below and around the M6 motorway in Birmingham at Spaghetti Junction.

Such action demonstrates that lay ministry, social responsibility and theological study are not three dimensions of the Church's life handled by different specialists at some church headquarters, but are in fact all one whole, seen from different perspectives. The same point is made by the Roman Catholic theologian Michael Winter. He examines the French pioneers who were so influential in the early days of Industrial Mission, and who are cited by Ted Wickham, Leslie Hunter and Margaret Kane. However, Winter believes that

> the prophetic aspirations of the French pioneers H. Godwin and G. Michonneau (with their books France: Pays de Mission (1943), translated into English as *France Pagan*, and Paroisse Communaute Missionaire (1945), translated into English as *Revolution in a City Parish*) have not been realised.[19]

They were defeated by the growing anonymity of urban life, and the traditional structure of the parishes. The parochial experiment at Stockton-on-Tees under Trevor Beeson in the 1950s produced remarkable community involvement. It is now a traditional Anglican parish. (Beeson's work predated Industrial Mission in Teesside by a few years.) However, Winter does not give up at this point. Instead he turns to the basic community movements, which have spread throughout the Third World. It is Winter's hope that these communities, which again are lay-led (though a priest may celebrate the Eucharist), study Scripture together and engage in social action, can spread across Europe as well. He is not optimistic, however, since he sees the great weakness of his own Church as being the nature of its authority, which has still not built a system of trust and confidence between the laity and those in power in the Church.

> Flattery is still rewarded, and authority is frequently seen to be powerless where punishment cannot be enforced. We have yet to achieve a system reposing upon trust and the ability to inspire confidence. There is, however, one way of hope. The laity cannot be coerced, and free speech has come to stay.[20]

There are three reasons why Winter opts for some form of basic community, all of them sociological. There is the pressure from social structures on human freedom, which limit the possibility of human responsibility; there is the weakness of the family in the face of mass leisure and the mass media; and the dichotomy between increased personal self-awareness and the inability to express this adequately. Basic communities give the possibility of freedom, responsibility and self-expression. Each one would be coterminous with one street in a city, or a block of flats, assisted by a priest who earned his own keep. Here the most important issue for Winter is the end of the clergy as a privileged class and their need to become as much as possible people who bear the ordinary responsibilities of life. He demonstrates at some length how in the early Church the clergy frequently earned their own keep. Winter therefore argues that until the insights of the 1980 Liverpool National Pastoral Congress, which argued for the development of small communities in each parish and a complete rethink of policy on clergy training to assist such communities, are actually accepted, little will happen.[21] Since the book was published, Michael Winter, who has published several books on mission in the period since the Second Vatican Council, has left his post as Dean of St Edmund's House, Cambridge. It is a serious loss to the Roman Catholic Church in England.

There are many other instances of lay ministry being developed. Robin Greenwood takes up the Vatican II stress on the baptized vocation of each Christian, though he is well aware that the development of a close-knit group of lay people, as described in 1 Peter 2:1–10, can become an inward-looking private club, quite unaware of the needs of mission. Yet ultimately he sees no conflict:

> It is one thing for church Councils to discuss mission, but quite another to be prepared radically to change their accustomed ways to create a psychological space into which a wide variety of people may enter and feel at home. An important way forward will be for churches increasingly to be led by local ministry teams, containing members both ordained and lay. Our planning needs to be biased towards making local churches more attractive and more available to more sections of society, without delay.[22]

It is a church with a community which assumes responsibility for itself, which does not have to fear for its future, for the decisions which it makes are its own. The issues raised by the women in Easington Colliery cannot be resolved simply by a more effective clerical ministry or by better social services. While these are important (and no past criticism at all is implied – precisely the opposite, in fact), and while a regeneration of the area's economy is much to be hoped for, in the long term community action and lay ministry must be the answer. Community action involves all those who have a stake in the future of the community; lay ministry is the vocation of the baptized to live out the good news of the Gospel for the sake of others. The theology of such a ministry is to act "in the service of God's work in the world".[23] Such a ministry will be a corporate one, wherein the ordained ministry focuses the activity of God in this corporate ministry into a particular pattern. Such a focusing requires the community to trust and sustain its ordained minister in faith, hope, integrity, vision and love, by which the minister recognizes the activity of God in the church community. Each therefore animates the other. But such a process of bringing each other to be, and so living out the performance of its mission, raises the most profound questions about the meaning of vision, trust and love. If community and pastoral work lead into the caring of the community of the church, and so into lay ministry, this in turn raises the question of what is meant by care. It is this which women in the Church have challenged most profoundly in recent years.

The Experience of Women

The literature about the place of women in the Church has grown dramatically in the last decade. Feminist theology, studies of women in the Christian tradition, feminist spirituality and forms of worship have all served to express a concern that the traditional attitude to women in the Church should change. There has also been an enormous outpouring of studies on the ordination of women to the priesthood, and on Christian attitudes to sexuality. In assessing the place of pastoral care in the Church's mission, what are the questions and new attitudes raised by women in the last few years? Even this could become a study in its own right, and any selection here must be limited.[24]

Anne Borrowdale takes up a theme often found in feminist literature. The woman is expected to provide the nurturing element in pastoral care, and to be passive and non-judgemental.[25] It is certainly here that this is an important part of the Christian response to others in need. Yet a whole host of problems lurk behind this assumption. First, how does this role relate to the ones which industrial chaplains may often need to adopt? There has been considerable discussion within Industrial Mission about the way in which that movement was in the past an all-male group. Secondly, there is the problem of stereotyping women by associating culturally conditioned roles with gender. There is no agreement at the moment as to how the terms "sex" and "gender" are used. Talk about gender characteristics plays on a confusion. The question is whether talk of gender characteristics is based on what is natural to the two sexes (the "essentialist" or "nature" view), or a product of "societal" norms (the "nurture" view), or a mixture of the two. Talk about "gender" in pastoral care thus turns out to be not only descriptive but also covertly prescriptive. Equally the argument becomes circular: since some women (or men) are good at a particular role, so all women (or men) should be.[26] Thirdly, there is the way in which we project on to one another what we are most uncomfortable with. It is clear that Christians are no better than other people at handling needs and demands, and find guilt all too common an emotion. Hugh Buckingham traces carefully the complexity which surrounds Christians who, in their attempts to do good, often end up in being regarded as hypocrites. Alistair Campbell examines how far the contrast between male and female responses to Jesus in the gospels exists, and Campbell concludes

> It is perhaps not surprising, then, that in the gospels it is women who are the ministers to Jesus, while the male disciples misunderstand him, fall asleep, or deny him at his time of greatest need. It is the women who offer a costly caring, though the men might equally be capable of it. It is the women whose bodily care gives comfort to Jesus while the men struggle for places of honour.[27]

Campbell therefore argues that "the 'sacrament' of caring is the use of the physical closeness of bodies to a therapeutic end, the overcoming of weakness and the rstoration of hope which another human presence makes possible". The crucial issue for ministry, of any sort, is to break down the "taboo on tenderness" which is so common in our society among men.[28] There is a theological answer to this *cultural* problem. Campbell cites Paul Tillich's account of acceptance which locates love in the most basic of human experiences, and yet shows the transcendent element of acceptance by God, which takes the individual beyond the confines of his or her own security. "Acceptance by God creates in us the possibility to accept and love others ... [Tillich describes] the doctrine of sin as estrangement and the doctrine of grace as acceptance."[29]

This means that the mission of the Church in evangelism, Industrial Mission and pastoral care now is faced with a great crisis of credibility if women's perceptions are not incorporated into what the Church is both saying and doing. It is not ultimately a question of the ordination of women to the priesthood, although that is certainly an issue as well. It is a question of how elements of femininity and caring can be accepted by men, while allowing women the ability to exercise authority and prophetic leadership as well. Mary Tanner, with long experience of ecumenical conversations, writes of her own participation as follows:

> The views and perspectives of women have too long been silent in our churches and when they are heard, the understanding of the unity of the churches is seen to go far beyond organizational unity and to be bound up with the healing of all divisions so that the church may become both a fitting sign and instrument in the renewal of human community.[30]

Why, it might be asked, does this affect evangelism? Mary Tanner points to the need to rethink the paradigm of divine self-giving, where God's love is not simply for those who conform to particular expectations. The new paradigm of divine self-giving is one which establishes freedom and calls people to join in Christ's offering. The obvious Biblical text is Philippians 2:7, where Christ "emptied himself taking the form of a servant". Letty Russell writes of the Pauline stress on the new reality in Christ in which we are called to live in freedom. The Pauline words in 1 Corinthians 7:25–31 are to live "as if not". The facts of the situation are not the end of the matter.[31] Much the same argument could be used of the Black experience in the Church as well.

There has been a great shift in writing about pastoral care since the 1950s. There was a tendency in their earlier writings for pastoral care to be seen as directed towards those who are weak, in crisis or with problems. But the implication can be that the pastor is the strong person (usually a strong, capable man, or shepherd) helping the weak. The shepherd stands above the problems which the dim-witted sheep are always falling into. More recently there has been much of a change, and the person who brings care is seen as someone who is also vulnerable and helpless. If the term "shepherd" is used, as it still is by Campbell, the reference is to the courage which the shepherd must show against the wolves: wolves of personal violence in the inner city, violence of despair and of complete social or economic collapse, as in Consett. In a 1988 Christmas sermon Timothy Radcliffe OP writes of the shepherds as wild, undomesticated people, who live on the edges of society outside the civilized world. Perhaps they were not included in the census of Luke 2. They do not count and they are not counted. Equally the birth of Christ was invisible to the powers of the ancient world, despite the searching of King Herod. However, it was the uncountable angels which proclaimed peace "for all people" to the uncounted shepherds. Only the angels and shepherds rejoiced over the birth of Jesus. Would we notice the shepherds today? asked Timothy Radcliffe. Or would they become invisible, much as the poor are invisible today in government statistics? Can we see in our society angels, shepherds, the poor or the birth of Christ? Radcliffe believes that the shepherds were poor and hungry, and sought an answer in the birth of Jesus. This is not seeing Jesus as the answer to every need, but it is to recognize the importance of a vision of what might be. When the steelworks closed in Consett, it was not easy to have a vision of the future. Why, asked Radcliffe, do we settle for so little? Why are we so afraid? It required a particular kind of courage to minister to steelworkers through a long year of social disintegration. In a striking comment, Richard Jones's acute survey of pastoral theology shows that not only does most pastoral theology assume that the pastor will be clerical and male, there is also no recognition of the place of the "Church Mother" in the black congregation who arranges caring and shares her authority with the pastor. (It is, of course, the case that this still associates caring with the woman, and that she is not the pastor.)[32]

Phyllis Anderson, a Lutheran American pastor, who spent some years in Durham, writes of the pastoral importance of women's leadership. The clear majority of her congregation are women, and there is an obvious and natural access into their lives. Yet, taking up the theme made by Dan Hardy and David Ford that mission is not simply about meeting needs or having a functional value, she also shows that her ministry can work with the strengths of her congregation, so that they can be "as strong and as smart and as powerful as God made us to be without sacrificing our faith or our families or our femininity". Yet it is not even as straightforward as this. As Ford and Hardy have stressed, mission is about enjoying the fullness of God. If all the worship is led by men – celebrant, preacher, reader, choir – then there can be no reflection of

> the fullness of the created order, the fullness of God. How would you ever guess by looking at such an all-male cast that all humanity, flesh and blood, body and spirit, male and female, were caught up in the body of Christ when God became incarnate in Jesus of Nazareth?[33]

Unity and Mission

In the Anglican–Roman Catholic International Commission (ARCIC) report on authority agreed in 1976, there is again an emphasis on the local church, although it is now taken into a wider vision of the whole Church. This book so far has not paid much attention to the wider Church, and it is time that this perspective is corrected. The Church is spoken of as a community seeking to submit to Christ. All in this community share in the life of the Spirit, and find within this community the means to be faithful to Christ. The Greek word for the common life is Koinonia, and it means a fundamental quality of the life of the Church: a communion of persons with God and with each other. Such a sharing in the Spirit is, says ARCIC,

> realized not only in the local Christian communities, but also in the communion of these communities with one another . . . Each local church is noted in the witness of the apostles and entrusted with the apostolic mission. Faithful to the Gospel, celebrating the one eucharist and dedicated to the service of the same Lord, it is the Church of Christ. In spite of diversities each local church recognizes its own essential features in the others and its true identity with them.[34]

ARCIC is quite clear that the mission of the Church to the world can never be the responsibility of each local church on its own, but must be that of all the local churches together. It also argues that the perception of God's will is a task for lay people and ordained ministry, for "all who live faithfully within the Koinonia may become sensitive to the leading of the Spirit and be brought towards a deeper understanding of the Gospel and of its implications in diverse cultures and changing situations". It is a process of "discernment and response, in which the faith is expressed and the Gospel is pastorally applied".[35]

ARCIC's vision is of all the local churches acting together. "The spiritual gifts of one may be an inspiration to the others." In a similar way the recent report on *communion and women in the Episcopate*, chaired by Archbishop Robert Eames, reads,

> Structures or bonds of communion, are the instruments for maintaining and strengthening the visible communion of the Church... All the various elements of visible communion are gifts of the risen Christ, through the power of the Holy Spirit, to the Church. They are not separable items but integrally related to one another. Working together they serve, and project the inner mystery of the Church's communion.[36]

Unity then is a mystery, which is related to growth in the Spirit, and is also desirable so that the Church may grow in the gifts of the Spirit. Authority in the Church is possible only through the action of the Spirit. It is through the common life in the body of Christ that men and women are equipped with what is needed to fulfil their responsibility and to act with authority. The responsibility is because of the universal leadership of Christ, which therefore gives the community "a responsibility towards all mankind, which demands participation in all that promotes the good of society and responsiveness to every form of human need".[37]

All this is placed in the ARCIC report under the pastoral oversight of the bishop, who "must ensure that the local community is distinctively Christian" and therefore "make it aware of the universal communion of which it is part".[38] For ARCIC there is a common strand which binds up authority, fellowship and unity in the local church. All these are related to the work of the Spirit in the local church, which unites local churches and makes mission possible. The Church of England response to the report spoke of "a double emphasis ... the need for Catholic unity focused in structures and persons transcending the local and [on] the need for a proper local diversity which must never be stifled".[39]

The problem of course is that many perceive that it has been stifled. This is not simply based on distrust of the Roman Catholic Curia. If all the weight of a mission theology is put upon the local church, as this book has done, and as at least arguably ARCIC did in its statement on authority, then the danger theologically is that each church becomes independent. Sociologically this is a recipe for sectarianism, while theologically it destroys the catholicity of the Church. Even if the catholicity of the Church is related, as I have proposed following Moltmann's theory of Church order, to the coming unity of the Kingdom, and to the boundless Lordship of Christ, nevertheless the unity of the Church is crucial.

If, however, the alternative is a repressive centralization or local church defiance of central authority, then the living memory of the Church is in danger of becoming a mere shadow of itself. The Eames Report argues for a "rich and God-given diversity" which manifests a unity in the power of the Spirit. That unity rests upon the revealed faith, which is the living memory of the Church constantly realized "in response to varying needs and circumstances": the living Tradition, of which the apostolic community was the first witness, alive to the memory of the exalted Christ. Schism for the Eames Report means that "separated groups interpret the Tradition over and against each other . . . all are impoverished, and the richness of diversity and unity which mirrors the inner life of God the Holy Trinity is subverted".[40]

The Eames Report therefore pleads for courtesy and respect, asking for a limit on the expression of dissent because of the need to have "a real commitment to the maintenance of the highest degree of communion".[41] Dissent in the case of Anglicanism refers to those who do not accept the ordination of women to the priesthood and the episcopate. Unfortunately the Roman Catholic interpretation of ARCIC, where a bishop has to ensure that a local church is distinctively Christian, means the opposite: Winter's book is a case-study in the marginalization of dissent. Stephen Sykes's article on ARCIC and the Papacy again shows the way in which there has been a great silencing of opposition to creative developments.[42] (Eames offers as a test of change a number of criteria: Does it make that Church more faithful to the Gospel? Can a church fulfil its mission more faithfully in its cultural context? Are there elements of continuity with the Church in other ages and different cultures? Does the development affect holiness of life? Does the Church continue to be seen as the Body of Christ, where the Gospel is proclaimed?[43])

Yet Stephen Sykes's view of the local church's place in the Roman Catholic Church is bleak:

> Leadership in the Church also needs to explore itself to an accurate flow of information from lay people in local communities. Neither critics nor lay opinion are invariably right; but if the critics have been silenced and the channels to the top have been carefully filtered so that leaders only hear what is known to please them, then talk of a sensus fidelium [common mind of the faithful] is a pious fraud.[44]

It is true that the local church in ARCIC means the unity of local communities under one bishop.[45] Nevertheless the Anglican–Reformed report *God's Reign and Our Unity* puts a caution against simply identifying the local church with a diocese:

> We have to take into account not only our church traditions, but the realities of the secular world in which the local Church must make its witness. Except in very simple static societies, modern communities consist of various overlapping groups whose members are related through language, work, culture and common interest. In order to be effective in missionary outreach the Church may have to encourage the formation of distinct groups in the same area. Yet these must be enabled to realise their unity through sharing the life of a diocese, presbytery or association. But even a large diocese, if it is small enough to have the real experience of unity, may be too small to embrace the life of a modern city.[46]

Disunity is bound to occur in the life of a church. Bishop David Jenkins of Durham repeatedly made headline news during events which this book describes. Bishop Jenkins argues that "there are no authentic grounds derivable from the story" to support the view that the churches are preserved from being obstacles to the story of Christianity. Churches frequently do "betray, distort and well-nigh deny the story".[47] Frequently the churches make the story "highly implausible and incredible". Therefore the loyalty of Bishop Jenkins is to the Kingdom of God. Church and Kingdom are interrelated in ways "subject to the vicissitudes and accidents of history". Nevertheless, Bishop Jenkins believes that there are a variety of ways in which the Church can serve the Kingdom. He abandons the possibility of a definite appeal to the past, due to the intolerance of the Church in the past; due to the end of the world in which religious claims made sense on their own; and due to the relativities of history. So for Bishop Jenkins revelation is always now or never.[48] He rejects the General Synod with its "smell of death. Elderly gentlemen, largely from within a decaying institution",[49] discussing irrelevant questions have no appeal for him. He prefers an appeal to a dynamic, pragmatic, experimental and provisional interrelationship of the churches,[50] where there is mutual accountability, provocation and collaboration. There is still an appeal to tradition, Scripture and worship, but it is focused on the tasks of the future. Therefore Bishop Jenkins looks with some uncertainty at the ecumenical agenda ("in your heart of hearts, do you think there is very much point in discussing the items on the agenda today?" Bishop Jenkins was asking his diocese to weigh up a discussion on ecumenical relations with the Chernobyl catastrophe which had just occurred).[51] "Can we find a way (I am not at all sure we can, but I think it is a proper question) by working with our ecumenical fellow Christians . . . ?"[52]

For others the ecumenical task, while difficult, is still necessary because of the need for local churches to preserve their unity together. It is striking that progress on both lay ministry and local developments is impeded by centralization in the Roman Catholic Church, however courageous and devoted many local parish clergy and laity are. There clearly need to be some criteria for new developments, and the balance between the local church (in the sense of the local community), the local diocese, other dioceses and the past tradition is never easy. Nevertheless, Anglicanism appears to have reached a breakdown in relationships at the international level, except perhaps with the Lutherans. It may be that the new successor to the British Council of Churches will revive that impetus: it is much to be hoped for.

Conclusion

We have moved a long way from the local co-operation of parish and specialist clergy, together with the lay Christians and non-Christians, who united in the face of the problems of Easington District. However, at the end of the day lay ministry and a greater role for women must not only be an essential pastoral strategy, they must also affect the relationship of the churches together. How churches respond to these developments while seeking to preserve that unity of the Spirit spoken of in ARCIC and in the Eames Report (and in both the Niagara Anglican–Lutheran report cited earlier in the book and the Anglican–Reformed one) is the crucial question. It is clear that mission is now seriously impeded by the suspicion some churches have of lay ministry and the ministry of women. It would be a tragedy if individual denominations, or local dioceses or church communities, were now to break apart. Yet the demands of mission are urgent, and the credibility of the Gospel does not gain by deferring action. What is needed is a way of taking the living tradition of the Church into the future by united action. Mission in the 1990s remains poised between disunity and lack of credibility. It is not a comforting prospect.

CONCLUSION

It is undeniably true that this book has been about places which are now remote from the centre of English life. It is striking that Easington District Council gave up advertising recently for a senior management position because after several attempts they had no suitable applicants. Easington, Consett, Sunderland are not typical of contemporary English society, nor is Newcastle-on-Tyne the same as many Southern cities.

Partly I wish to affirm the cultural variety which this brings, and I hope that my immense affection for the area has been shown in this book. Yet at the same time

> the decline of Labour's traditional social base continues relentlessly. Home ownership goes on growing, the class desegregation of communities proceeds, so does movement from city to suburb, small town and country. The declining industries decline, large scale gives way to smaller, mass-production to high-tech, unionisation to non-unionisation, and with all these changes dies an ethos as a world disappears.[1]

This book has been written from a very specific viewpoint, and that vantage-point is increasingly becoming marginal to English society. No one knows how this area will look in twenty-five years' time. Yet the reason for taking a particular vantage-point was to argue theologically for certain understandings of mission. It is, I have argued, important that mission is the engagement of the local church with its community. To be aware of the complexity of that community today requires a grasp of the sociology of religion, even if at the same time stories are told about the local church, people in the local community or dramatic social changes. Sociology of religion uses theoretical concepts; stories are about people's accounts of their daily experiences. Yet the surveys carried out by Francis and Hornby-

Smith, or the work of Martin and others, can only be prolegomena to a theology of mission, as they would be the first to argue themselves.

There is much that has been omitted in this book. The suggestions by Leslie Francis and Frank Field MP about church schools deserve examination, even if the danger is that of a sectarian Christianity. Church schools have long been undervalued in the Anglican context as a tool for mission and building up the faith. There has been nothing in this book either about non-stipendiary ministers, who work at secular jobs by day (or night, if on shift-work) and exercise their ministry both at work and in their parishes. Most strikingly there has been nothing on inter-faith dialogue, or the mission of the Church overseas. On the latter, it seems to me now that while the Western Church has technical skills and a long tradition of service to offer to the Church in the Third World, and while the two-way interchange of personnel helps the fellowship of the Church, it is no longer relevant to the task of the Church in England to look at the missionary task in Africa. Of course there will be insights each can bring to bear on the other's situation, and that is why an interchange of visitors should go on. However, there are now two different worlds, each with their own needs. As for inter-faith dialogue, I can only plead that such a vast subject, of so great importance, deserves a book of its own. The relationship of Christianity to Islam, Hinduism, Sikhism and Buddhism cannot be included under the general title of "inter-faith dialogue". Judaism is different, which is why I have mentioned it on several occasions in this book. I realize that there is a pressing need for the local church to come to terms with a multi-cultural, interfaith world, and the work of such people as Sam Prasadam with the "Westenders" project in West Newcastle deserves the greatest support. This project concerned the dialogue of people of different faiths in the same community. Space has prevented any discussion of it here.

So where does the future of mission lie, before "the decade of evangelism" which the General Synod of the Church of England has called Anglicans to engage in during the 1990s?

> The Church is the concrete place where certain human beings accept a call to associate with Christ, the reality of Him who is the expression and embodiment of divine love. This association is for the rest of humanity ... In the Church Jesus Christ, Son of God and our Saviour, can be said to take form and achieve present reality for the world. The importance of Christ's significance for the world is a practical one. As the Church is taken up into the love of God it becomes that love for all the world. Christ is divine and human: he offers God's love in the Church for everyone. This means that the issues of practical Christianity, the Church and the nature of God become a whole ... What sort of form does the church have? It is only a Church insofar as it is based on the present reality of Jesus. The Church is the place where God's love that is Jesus takes form in the present, and insofar as it does God's love is real for the world.[2]

The implications for mission and theology are quite precise. Mission is about involving local people at a particular time and place in particular issues, whether of pastoral care, economic realities or the love of God shown in the life of the Church. Such involvement must be related to the theological tradition. Theology is part of the process of reflecting upon our common Christian faith, enabling local people to be themselves and to engage in depth with the contemporary situation. It is a total response, which cannot be divided into a concern with ecumenism, evangelism, social concern or Biblical studies. That response is always surrounded and supported by the reality of the self-giving of God's love, to which the Church responds in adoration and thanks. Drawing people into that response, by setting out the attractiveness of that love, beauty and truth which is the activity of God, is what evangelism is all about. Ultimately

I have argued that a community which is responding to that love will have a compelling quality about its own life. Yet such a community cannot be divorced from the reality of daily life. That is why I have explored at some length the literature which discusses the future of Industrial Mission. Pastoral care is also an aspect of the Christian life which many recent theologians have written about, and I have sought to discuss a little of their work. Mission is the local Church being the Body of Christ in its neighbourhood. It is as simple and as complex as that.

NOTES

Chapter 1

1. S. Hauerwas, *The Peaceable Kingdom*, SCM 1983, p. 33.

2. R. Greenwood, *Reclaiming the Church*, Fount 1988, p. 32.

3. A. T. Hanson, *Church, Sacraments and Ministry*, Mowbrays 1975, pp. 113–14. Hanson of course is basing his argument on R. C. Moberly's *Ministerial Priesthood*, 1897.

4. D. Isitt, *Look for the Living*, Epworth 1989, p. 26.

5. J. Moltmann, *The Church in the Power of the Spirit*, SCM 1977, p. 43.

6. Moltmann, op. cit., p. 337.

7. J. and A. Pearce, *Inner City Spirituality*, Grove Spirituality Series, No. 21, 1987.

8. H. Willmer, "Politview I. Faith in the City", *Modern Churchman*, Vol. XXVIII No. 3 (1986), pp. 12–13.

9. L. Green, *Power to the Powerless*, Marshall Pickering 1987, p. 119.

10. S. Hauerwas, op. cit., p. 148.

11. J. Dunn (ed.), *The Kingdom of God and North-East England*, SCM 1986, pp. 45–8.

Chapter 2

1. B. Wilson, *Religion in Secular Society*, Watts 1966.

2. D. Martin, *The Religious and the Secular*, Routledge 1969; *A General Theory of Secularization*, Blackwell 1978; *The Dilemmas of Contemporary Religion*, 1978; *The Social Context of Theology*, Mowbrays 1975; *Theology and Social Structure*, Mowbrays 1977; *Beyond Decline*, SCM 1988.

3. Martin, *The Religious and the Secular*, p. 94.

4. Martin, op. cit., p. 95.

5. *The Northern Echo*, 10 Feburary 1987.

6. Martin, *The Religious and the Secular*.

7. Don Cupitt, *The New Christian Ethics*, SCM 1988, p. 169.

8. John Habgood, *Confessions of a Conservative Liberal*, SPCK 1988, p. 7.

9. Augustine, *Confessions*, 7. 20.

10. John Riches, *Jesus and the Transformation of Judaism*, DLT 1980, p. 75.

11. J. Dunn, *The Kingdom of God in North-East England*, SCM 1986, p. 6; C. Rowland, *Christian Origins*, SPCK 1985.

12. D. Senior and C. Stuhlmueller, *The Biblical Foundations for Mission*, SCM 1983, p. 242.

13. Martin, *The Religious and the Secular*, p. 67; J. Habgood, *Church and Nation in a Secular Age*, DLT 1983, pp. 80–85.

14. Habgood, *Church and Nation in a Secular Age*, p. 81.

Chapter 3

1. Phil Brown, "God in Sunderland", Aston Training Scheme Project 1988.

2. Hazel Ditchburn, "Scotswood", William Temple Foundation, Manchester, Certificate in Religious Studies Project 1987.

3. L. Francis, *Monitoring the Christian Development of the Child*, Culham College Institute 1986. See also his *Teenagers and the Church*, Collins 1984.

4. L. Francis, *Church and School – a Future for Christian Education*, Culham College Institute 1986.

5. M. Winter, *Whatever Happened to Vatican Two?*, Sheed and Ward 1985, p. 87.

6. Winter, op. cit., p. 96.

7. Winter, op. cit., pp. 94–5.

8. John Habgood, *Church and Nation in a Secular Age* p. 32.

9. A. Houpeten, *People of God*, SCM 1983.

10. Houpeten, op. cit., p. 5.

11. Houpeten, op. cit., pp. 12–13.

12. M. Saward, *Evangelicals on the Move*, Mowbrays 1986.

13. Peter Baelz, *Prayer and Providence*, Seabury, New York, 1968.

Chapter 4

1. A. Houpeten, *People of God*, p. 16. Engl. translation 1984.

2. Francis Penhale, *Catholics in Crisis?*, Mowbrays 1986.

3. A. Archer, *The Two Catholic Churches*, SCM 1986.

4. J. Habgood. *Confessions of a Conservative Liberal*, p. 8.

5. Habgood, op. cit., p. 26.

6. Habgood, op. cit., p. 63.

7. The US Roman Catholic Bishops, *The Challenge of Peace. God's Promise and Our Response*, CTS/SPCK 1983, paras. 51–3.

8. Dan Hardy and David Ford, *Jubilate – Theology in Praise*, DLT 1984, p. 150.

9. Hardy and Ford, op. cit., p. 143.

10. Hardy and Ford, op. cit., p. 74.

11. W. H. Vanstone, *Love's Endeavour, Love's Expense*, DLT 1977, p. 96.

12. Vanstone, op. cit., p. 96.

13. Vanstone, op. cit., p. 97.

14. Vanstone, op. cit., p. 14.

15. Vanstone, op. cit., p. 108.

16. Vanstone, op. cit., p. 114.

17. Vanstone, op. cit., p. 71.

18. Anglican/Lutheran International Continuation Committee, *The Niagara Report*, LWF/SPCK 1987, para. 22.

19. Vanstone, op. cit., p. 119.

20. S. Hauerwas, *The Peaceable Kingdom*, SCM 1984, p. 107.

21. Hauerwas, op. cit., p. 102.

22. Hauerwas, op. cit., p. 98.

23. Hauerwas, op. cit., p. 102.

24. Hauerwas, op. cit., p. 110.

25. Hauerwas, op. cit., p. 148.

26. G. Lindbeck, "The Church" in *Keeping the Faith*, ed. G. Wainwright, SPCK 1989, p. 179.

27. Lindbeck, op. cit., p. 183.

28. Lindbeck, op. cit., p. 185.

29. Lindbeck, op. cit., p. 193.

30. Lindbeck, op. cit., p. 194.

31. Lindbeck, op. cit., p. 204.

32. Lindbeck, op. cit., p. 205.

33. Lindbeck, op. cit., p. 204.

34. Lindbeck, op. cit., p. 193.

35. G. Lindbeck, *The Nature of Doctrine*, SPCK 1984, p. 33.

36. Lindbeck, *The Nature of Doctrine*, p. 126.

37. Don Cuppitt, *The New Christian Ethics*, SCM 1988; R. Green, *Only Connect*, DLT 1987; Philip Toynbee, *Towards the Holy Spirit*, SCM; David Cockerell, *Beginning Where We Are*, SCM 1989.

38. For further treatment of this point, see Peter Sedgwick, "Mass Media and Mass Culture", *Crucible*, July 1989.

39. Lindbeck, *The Nature of Doctrine*, p. 127.

40. Lindbeck, "The Church", p. 194.

41. Lindbeck, "The Church", p. 194.

42. Lindbeck, "The Church", p. 188.

43. Lindbeck, "The Church", p. 195.

44. R. H. Roberts, "Spirit, Structure and Truth in the Church", *Modern Theology*, Vol. III No. 1 (October 1986); S. Tugwell, *Did you Receive the Spirit?*, London, 1972; J. V. Taylor, *The Go-Between God, The Holy Spirit and Christian Mission*, London, 1972.

45. Roberts, op. cit., p. 94.

46. Roberts, op. cit., p. 103.

47. Nicholas Lash, "The Politics of Evangelization in Britain Today", *Church Action on Poverty*, Network 11 (spring 1989), p. 9. (Network 11 equals Vol. X, No. 9.)

48. *City and Church – A Century of Movement*, 21 November 1982.

49. *Baptism, Eucharist and Ministry*, World Council of Churches, Geneva, 1982, Ministry 1–2.

Chapter 5

1. John Eyles, *Diary of a Closure*. BSC Consett Works, December 1979–December 1980, Northumbrian Industrial Mission.

2. Fred Robinson (ed.), *Post-Industrial Tyneside*, Newcastle-upon-Tyne City Library and Arts 1988, p. 212.

3. *IM – An Appraisal. The Church's Response to the Changing Industrial and Economic Order*, Church of England Board for Social Responsibility 1988.

4. G. Hewitt (ed.), *Strategist for the Spirit: Leslie Hunter,*

Bishop of Sheffield 1939–1962, Beckett Publications 1985.

5. M. Davies, "Industrial Mission – the Way Ahead?" *ICF Quarterly*, autumn 1988.

6. E. R. Wickham, *Church and People in an Industrial City*, Lutterworth 1957, p. 221.

7. Wickham, op. cit., p. 253.

8. *Changing Industrial Mission: Models and Hopes.* Industrial Mission Association Theology Development Group 1985, p. 2.

9. C. Beales, "Are Issues too Easy?", *IMA Newsletter*, August 1984.

10. *Thinking in Practice: Theology and Industrial Mission.* Industrial Mission Association Theology Development Group; David Welbourn, "Industrial Chaplains – Yesterday and Today", *ICF Quarterly*, summer 1988; M. Kane, *What Kind of God?*, SCM 1986; M. Davies, "The Church's Response to the Changing Industrial and Economic Order", *Crucible*, January 1987; J. Hammersley, "Chrisianity and the Metro Centre do not Mix", *Crucible*, April 1988; A. Borrowdale, "Women and the Theology of Work", *Crucible*, October 1985; M. Grundy, "Can we Say 'Thanks to Industry'?", *Crucible*, January 1986; The Industrial Committee of the Church of England's Board for Social Responsibility has also issued six papers: S. Masumoto, *A Critique of British Industrial Mission*; P. Sedgwick, *Not Ceasing from Exploring*; J. Eagle, *A Smouldering Land* (on the Philippines); K. Muir, *Industrial Mission – Catholic Style*; C. Beales, *Tools for Fools*, Pt 1; C. Beales, *Tools for Fools*, Pt 2.

11. Hewitt, op. cit., p. 157.

12. Davies, *ICF Quarterly*, autumn 1988.

13. Davies, *Crucible*, January 1987.

14. Kane, op. cit., p. 9.

15. The two earlier books are *Theology in an Industrial Society*, 1975, and *Gospel in Industrial Society*, 1980.

16. Kane, *What Kind of God?*, p. 40.

17. Kane, *What Kind of God?*, p. 35.

18. Kane, *What Kind of God?*, p. 52.

19. Kane, *What Kind of God?*, p. 68, citing J. M. Bonino, *Revolutionary Theology Comes of Age*, SPCK 1975, p. 167.

20. Kane, *What Kind of God?*, pp. 85–7, citing J. L. Segundo, *The Liberation of Theology*, Gill 1977.

21. Kane, *What Kind of God?*, p. 84.

22. Kane, *What Kind of God?*, p. 123.

23. Kane, *What Kind of God?*, p. 52.

24. "We are all indebted in this field to the life and writings of Margaret Kane" – John Atherton, *Thinking in Practice – Theology and Industrial Mission*, p. 98.

25. *IM – An Appraisal*, p. 91, citing Kane, *What Kind of God?*, p. 117.

26. IM – An Appraisal, p. 9.

27. IM – An Appraisal, p. 48.

28. IM – An Appraisal, p. 88.

29. IM – An Appraisal, p. 108.

30. P. H. Sedgwick, *Not Ceasing from Exploring*, pp. 28–34, gives a longer account of this argument.

31. J. Atherton, *Faith in the Nation*, SPCK 1988. For a brief account of his views, see his ICF 1988 lecture.

32. Malcolm Torry's review of *Not Ceasing from Exploring* argues this point strongly. See *IMA Newsletter*, September 1987.

33. N. Lash, *Theology on the Way to Emmaus*, SCM 1986, p. 44.

Chapter 6

1. *Coal, Church and Community*, Theological Consultancy to the North-East Churches/Environmental Services Department, Easington District Council, Easington, Co. Durham SR8 3TN 1986.

2. Undermining Easington, University of Durham, Department of Geography, December 1984.

3. *Northern Region of England*, Profile 1989 – Northern Region Councils Association, Newcastle, 1989; *It's not really like that* (living with unemployment in the North-

East). A report for BBC North-East, by Fred Robinson, University of Newcastle on Tyne, March 1987.

4. Townsend, pp. 63 and 77.

5. Townsend, p. 79.

6. Townsend, p. 82.

7. Townsend, p. 159.

8. Townsend, p. 179.

9. Townsend, op. cit., p. 79.

10. *The Last Coals of Spring*, Durham Voices, 1985.

11. J. O'Keefe in *Coal, Church and Community*, p. 67.

12. Paul Ballard, "Community Work and Mission", *Modern Churchman*, Vol. XXVIII No. 3 (1986), pp. 35–40.

13. See also E. Graham, "The Pastoral Significance of Community Work", *Modern Churchman*, Vol. XXX No. 2 (1988), and Paul Ballard, *In and Out of Work: A Pastoral Perspective*, St Andrews Press 1987.

14. S. W. Sykes, "Hope and Health", *Crucible*, January 1980 (address given in Sunderland in 1979 to the Annual Conference of the Institute of Religion and Medicine).

15. Sykes, op. cit., p. 17.

16. Sykes, op. cit., p. 15.

17. Peter Baelz, *The Forgotten Dream*, Mowbrays 1975, p. 142.

18. Green, *Power to the Powerless*, pp. 50–87.

19. Winter, *Whatever Happened to Vatican II?*, p. 150.

20. Winter, op. cit., p. 86.

21. Winter, op. cit., pp. 62–74.

22. R. Greenwood, *Reclaiming the Church*, Collins Fount 1988, p. 156, and "Support for the Strong", *Theology*, September 1987. See also, for practical suggestions, Ronald Metcalfe, *Sharing Christian Ministry*, Mowbrays 1981.

23. *Education for the Church's Ministry*, ACCM Paper No. 22, Church of England General Synod 1987.

24. R. G. Jones, "On Dispensing with Shepherds?", *Modern Churchman*, Vol. XXV No. 2 (1982); Phyllis Anderson, "Both Kinds of Pastor", *Modern Churchman*, Vol. XXV No. 2 (1982); Mary Tanner, "A Chance to Change", *Modern Churchman*, Vol. XXV No. 3 (1983); Anne Borrowdale, "The Church as Equal Opportunity's Employer", *Crucible*, April 1988; Anne Borrowdale, "Women and the Theology of Work", *Crucible*, October 1985; Anne Borrowdale, *A Woman's Work – Changing Christian Attitudes*, SPCK 1989; Monica Furlong (ed.), *Mirror to the Church*, SPCK 1988; G. Anderson (ed.), *Mission Trends No. 4*, Paulist, New York, 1979.

25. Borrowdale, *Crucible*, 1988, p. 66.

26. S. Coakley, "'Femininity' and the Holy Spirit?" in Furlong (ed.), *Mirror to the Church*, p. 131.

27. Alastair Campbell, *Professional Care*, Fortress Press 1984, p. 110.

28. Hugh Buckingham, *How to be a Christian in Trying Circumstances*, Epworth 1985, p. 100. See also his *Feeling Good*, Epworth 1989.

29. Campbell, op. cit., p. 74. The citation of Paul Tillich is of his *Love, Power and Justice*, 1954.

30. Tanner, op. cit., p. 29.

31. Letty M. Russell, 'Women and Freedom", in G. Anderson (ed.), *Mission Trends No. 3*, p. 242.

32. Jones, op. cit.

33. Anderson, op. cit.

34. Anglican–Roman Catholic International Commission, *The Final Report*, CTS/SPCK 1982, Authority 1 III. 8.

35. ARCIC, Authority 1 III. 6.

36. *Report of the Archbishop of Canterbury's Commission on Communion and Women in the Episcopate* (The Eames Report), ACC/Church House Publishing 1989, paras. 13 and 14.

37. ARCIC, Authority 1 I. 3.

38. ARCIC, Authority 1 III. 8.

39. *Towards a Church of England Response to BEM and ARCIC*, Faith and Order Advisory Group, Board for Mission and Unity, Church House Publishing 1985, p. 98.

40. Eames Report, para. 15.

41. Eames Report, para. 31.

42. S. W. Sykes, "ARCIC and the Papacy", *Modern Churchman*, Vol. XXV No. 1 (1982).

43. Eames Report, para. 34.

44. Sykes, op. cit., p. 12.

45. ARCIC, Authority 1 III. 8.

46. Anglican–Reformed International Commission, *God's Reign and Our Unity*, SPCK 1984, p. 79, para. 111.

47. David E. Jenkins, *God, Miracle and the Church of England*, SCM, p. 94.

48. Jenkins, op. cit., p. 100.

49. Jenkins, op. cit., p. 101.

50. Jenkins, op. cit., p. 106.

51. Jenkins, Durham Diocesan Synod Presidential Address, 10 May 1986.

52. Jenkins, *God, Miracle and the Church of England*, p. 108.

Conclusion

1. Peter Jenkins, *The Independent*, 13 July 1989.

2. The Theological Consultancy to the North-East Ecumenical Group: A Final Report, May 1988.